PC BAS

for Beginners

PC BASIC

for Beginners

Brian D. Hahn

Edward Arnold
A division of Hodder & Stoughton
LONDON   BALTIMORE   MELBOURNE   AUCKLAND

© 1988 B. D. Hahn

First published in Great Britain 1988

British Library Cataloguing Publication Data

Hahn, Brian D.
 PC Basic for beginners.
 1. IBM PC microcomputer systems.
 Programming languages. Basic language -
 Manuals
 I. Title
 005.2'65

ISBN 0-7131-3586-7

All rights reserved. No part of this publication may be reproduced or transmitted in any form or by any means, electronically or mechanically, including photocopying, recording or any information storage or retrieval system, without either the prior permission in writing from the publisher or a licence permitting restricted copying. In the United Kingdom such licences are issued by the Copyright Licensing Agency: 33–34 Alfred Place, London WC1E 7DP.

Printed and bound in Great Britain for Edward Arnold, the educational academic and medical publishing division of Hodder and Stoughton Limited, 41 Bedford Square, London WC1B 3DQ by J. W. Arrowsmith, Bristol.

PREFACE

So many books on BASIC have been written that the appearance of yet another one seems to require some justification. There are three particular areas where this book can claim to make a distinctive contribution. Firstly, the version of BASIC in the text is Microsoft BASIC Release 2.0, which runs on "IBM compatible" personal computers, and is therefore likely to be very widely used. Secondly, the approach taken is a problem solving one, developed over many years of teaching computer programming to first year university students. The computer is presented as a tool for solving interesting real world problems, and examples from a number of areas are discussed. Thirdly, a deliberate attempt is made to develop clear, structured programs; the beginner is shielded from the devastating GOTO statement until well into the text, by which time he has been introduced to more sober habits (in fact, he can do without it altogether!). Emphasis is also laid on what has come to be called programming style.

This book is based on material prepared for applied mathematics students with no prior computing experience. As such it is intended to be a "teach yourself" guide to anyone intent on learning BASIC programming. It is not meant to be an exhaustive treatise on the subject: it is meant to launch you safely on the way to discovering more about this fascinating subject for yourself.

No mathematical background is needed in order to follow most of the examples. There are occasional forays into high school and first year university mathematics, but these may be glossed over without loss of continuity (you may even find them instructive!).

Finally, it should be stressed that computer programming cannot be mastered merely by reading (and learning) a book. It must be practised. There are consequently many worked examples and exercises thoughout the text and it should be your aim to program and run them successfully on a computer yourself as soon as possible.

I wish to thank John Newmarch, of the University of Cape Town Information Technology Services, for introducing me to many of the concepts of programming style presented in this book. Thanks are also due to my colleagues Kathy Pay and Christie Feros, on whom the manuscript was (successfully!) tested, for carefully "debugging" it. I would also like to thank my wife, Cleone, for her continual support and encouragement during the preparation of this book.

Brian D. Hahn
1987

CONTENTS

1. GETTING GOING — 1
  1.1. Why BASIC? — 1
  1.2. Running Simple BASIC Programs — 2
  1.2.1. Introducing Yourself to the Computer — 2
  1.2.2. Adding Two Numbers — 3
  1.2.3. Compound Interest — 3
  1.3. More Readable Programs and Output — 5
  1.3.1. The REM Statement — 5
  1.3.2. Inline Comments — 6
  1.3.3. A More Readable Example — 6
  1.3.4. Re-arranging Output with PRINT — 6
  1.3.5. Programming Style — 7
  1.4. Handling Program Files on Diskettes — 7
  1.5. BASIC Commands — 8
  1.6. EXERCISE — 9

2. ELEMENTARY BASIC — 10
  2.1. Line Format — 10
  2.2. Arithmetic in BASIC — 10
  2.2.1. Constants — 10
  2.2.2. Variables — 11
  2.2.3. Example: Vertical Motion under Gravity — 12
  2.2.4. Assignment Statements — 12
  2.2.5. Arithmetic Operators — 13
  2.2.6. Precedence of Operations — 13
  2.3. The INPUT Statement — 14
  2.3.1. Example: Future Value of an Investment — 15
  2.4. Repeating with FOR-NEXT: Compound Interest — 15
  2.5. Example: Final Course Mark — 17
  2.6. Deciding with IF-THEN-ELSE — 18
  2.7. The READ-DATA Statements — 20
  2.8. String Variables — 21
  2.8.1. Assignment of Strings — 21
  2.8.2. Strings as Data — 21
  2.8.3. Concatenation of Strings — 22
  2.9. EXERCISES — 23

3. PROGRAM PREPARATION — 26
  3.1. Flowcharting Symbols — 26
  3.2. Student Mark Problem — 28
  3.3. Company Payroll — 29
  3.4. Largest Number in a List — 30
  3.5. Structure Plans — 31
  3.6. EXERCISES — 32

4. STRUCTURED PROGRAMS: GOSUB — 33

4.1. The GOSUB Statement	33
4.2. Example: Company Payroll	34
4.3. Example: Largest Number in a List	35
4.4. EXERCISES	36

5. LOOPS 37
5.1. Conditional Loops	37
5.2. The WHILE and WEND Statements	39
5.3. Summary: When to Repeat with WHILE-WEND	39
5.4. Repeating with IF-GOTO	40
5.5. Looping with FOR-NEXT	40
5.5.1. Factorials	40
5.5.2. The Binomial Coefficient	41
5.5.3. General	41
5.6. Example: Newton's Method to Find a Square Root	42
5.7. Example: Vertical Motion under Gravity	43
5.8. Example: Regular Repayment of a Loan	43
5.9. Example: Computing the Limit of a Sequence	44
5.10. Summary: When to Repeat with FOR-NEXT	45
5.11. EXERCISES	45

6. SPECIAL FUNCTIONS 47
6.1. List of Special Functions	47
6.2. Example: Projectile Motion	48
6.3. EXERCISES	49

7. ERRORS 50
7.1. Syntax Errors	50
7.2. Execution Errors	51
7.3. Rounding Error	52
7.4. Errors of Logic	53

8. ADVANCED INPUT/OUTPUT 54
8.1. PRINT USING: Numeric Fields	54
8.1.1. The # Formatting Character	54
8.1.2. The + Formatting Character	55
8.1.3. The $$ Formatting Characters	55
8.1.4. Exponential Format	55
8.1.5. The — Formatting Character	56
8.2. PRINT USING: String Fields	56
8.2.1. The ! Formatting Character	56
8.2.2. The \\ Formatting Characters	56
8.3. The LPRINT USING Statement	56
8.4. Files: Updating Student Records	56
8.4.1. Sending Output to a File: WRITE #	57
8.5. EXERCISE	60

9. ARRAYS — 61
- 9.1. Mean and Standard Deviation — 61
- 9.2. Bar Charts and Frequency Distributions — 62
- 9.3. Sorting a List: the Bubble Sort — 64
- 9.3.1. Sorting Strings — 66
- 9.4. Order of Merit List — 67
- 9.5. Top of the Class — 68
- 9.6. Updating Student Records Again — 68
- 9.7. A Basic Budget — 72
- 9.8. Postscript — 75
- 9.9. EXERCISES — 75

10. SIMULATION — 77
- 10.1. Rolling a Fair Die — 77
- 10.2. Simulating Bacteria Division — 78
- 10.3. Spinning a Fair Coin — 79
- 10.4. A Random Walk — 79
- 10.5. Traffic Flow — 80
- 10.6. Dealing a Bridge Hand — 83
- 10.7. Queues — 85
- 10.8. EXERCISES — 88

11. USER DEFINED FUNCTIONS — 90
- 11.1. The DEF FN Statement — 90
- 11.2. Example: Newton's Method Again — 91
- 11.3. EXERCISE — 91

12. SPECIAL TEXT AND GRAPHICS FACILITIES — 92
- 12.1. Text Mode — 92
- 12.2. Medium Resolution Colour Graphics — 93
- 12.2.1. Example: Traffic Lights — 93
- 12.2.2. Example: Repayment of a Loan — 94
- 12.2.3. Example: Chook-Puff Animation — 95
- 12.3. High Resolution Graphics — 96
- 12.3.1. Example: Angle of Launch for Maximum Range — 96
- 12.4. Graphs on the Line Printer — 97
- 12.5. EXERCISES — 99

13. MATRICES — 100
- 13.1. A Concrete Example — 100
- 13.2. Matrix Multiplication — 102
- 13.3. Transformation of a Co-ordinate System — 104
- 13.4. Reachability Matrix of a Network — 105
- 13.5. Calculation of Volumes of Excavation — 108
- 13.6. Area of a Site — 110
- 13.7. Special MAT Statements — 112

14. INTRODUCTION TO NUMERICAL METHODS 115
   14.1. Equations 115
   14.1.1. Newton's Method 115
   14.1.2. Example: Hire Purchase Rip-off 117
   14.1.3. The Bisection Method 119
   14.2. Integration 121
   14.2.1. The Trapezoidal Rule 122
   14.3. Numerical Differentiation 124
   14.4. First Order Differential Equations 125
   14.4.1. Euler's Method 126
   14.4.2. Bacteria Growth 129
   14.4.3. A Predictor Corrector Method 131
   14.5. Runge-Kutta Methods 132
   14.5.1. Runge-Kutta Third Order Formula 132
   14.5.2. A Predator Prey Model 132
   14.6. EXERCISES 134

APPENDIX A: PROGRAMMING STYLE 136

APPENDIX B: SUMMARY OF BASIC STATEMENTS 137

APPENDIX C: SUMMARY OF BASIC COMMANDS 149

APPENDIX D: RESERVED WORDS 153

APPENDIX E: SUMMARY OF BASIC FUNCTIONS 154

APPENDIX F: ASCII CHARACTER CODES 161

APPENDIX G: USING THE KEYBOARD 163
Editing a Program 163
Special Function Keys 163
BASIC Keywords 164

APPENDIX H: SOLUTIONS TO SELECTED PROBLEMS 166

INDEX 175

CHAPTER 1

1 GETTING GOING

You are probably familiar with using an electronic calculator to find numerical answers to arithmetic problems. The simplest sort can only do arithmetic and display an answer. The next step up is one with a single memory — where an intermediate result may be stored — and with function keys, such as sin, cos, log, etc. Even better calculators may have a number of memory locations, so that many different intermediate results may be stored during a long and involved calculation.

However, if you have to perform the same sequence of operations on a calculator many times for different sets of data, it can become extremely tedious. So even more sophisticated calculators allow you to store, in some suitable coded form on a magnetic card, the sequence of operations (or instructions) needed to calculate the solution of the problem. This sequence of instructions is called a program. To carry out the entire set of calculations, you need only load the program into the calculator, press the "run" key, provide the necessary data, and sit back while the calculator churns out the answer. A calculator like this is described as programmable.

A computer, whether it is a mainframe or a microcomputer, is really only an advanced programmable calculator, capable of executing and storing sets of instructions, called programs, in order to solve specific problems.

1.1. Why BASIC?

The particular set of rules or conventions for coding the instructions to the computer is called a programming language. There are many such languages, e.g. BASIC, FORTRAN and Pascal. The aim of this book is to enable you to solve interesting, relevant problems using BASIC programming. BASIC, which stands for Beginner's All-purpose Symbolic Instruction Code, was developed by John Kemeny and Thomas Kurtz at Dartmouth College, U.S.A. The first BASIC program was run on a General Electric 225 computer at 4 a.m. on 1st May 1964, and the world of computing has never been the same since! The major advantage of BASIC is that it is by far the easiest programming language to learn, as is evidenced by the vast number of children who use it successfully. In 1978 Kurtz estimated that five million schoolchildren had learnt BASIC. Galanter (1983) reports that seven and eight year-olds are learning to write simple BASIC programs at his computer school for children.

Another advantage of BASIC is that it is the language used by the vast majority of microcomputers flooding into offices, shops, factories, schools, universities and homes all over the world, and so a good knowledge of BASIC enhances the employment prospects of anyone entering a career in any of these areas.

There are many different versions of BASIC. The one used in this book is Microsoft BASIC release 2.0, as supported by "IBM compatible" personal computers.

1.2. Running Simple BASIC Programs

The object of this section is to get you running some simple BASIC programs on your computer system without necessarily at first understanding how the programs work. Detailed explanations will follow in due course.

1.2.1. *Introducing Yourself to the Computer*

Seat yourself comfortably in front of the computer, and switch it on. The power switch is usually in some inaccessible place, like behind the machine. This is deliberate, so that you cannot accidentally switch it off, and lose everything in your current session that you might not have saved. If you have a diskette version of BASIC, put the "System Disk" into the disk drive (drive A if there is more than one). After the machine has whirred and clicked for a while, it may, depending on your particular system, put you directly into BASIC, or it may end up displaying the "system prompt"

A>

which means it is ready for you to do something. Type the word BASIC and press the RETURN key (denoted in this book by the ® symbol). When the computer is finally ready to run BASIC programs, the BASIC prompt

Ok

is displayed. Type in the following program, one line at a time, pressing ® at the end of each line (information on the screen is only communicated to the computer once ® has been pressed):

```
10   INPUT "What is your name"; N$
20   PRINT "Hi there,"; N$
30   END
```

That's a three line BASIC program. Now type RUN (or press the RUN function key if your computer has one). The computer should ask you for your name. Type your name, followed by ®, and it should greet you by name. (This is called an "interactive" program, because you and the computer interact: it waits for you to type your name before proceeding.)

At this stage the "Ok" prompt should be displayed again. RUN the program again, and this time mis-spell your name, or give it a different name, and see what happens. Now change the semi-colon in line 20 to a comma (either re-enter line 20, or consult Appendix G on how to edit a BASIC line) and RUN to see what difference this makes. Next change the PRINT in line 20 to LPRINT, and RUN again (make sure your computer's printer is connected and switched on!). Now change the LPRINT back to PRINT, and experiment with the **Ctrl/PrtSc** and **Shift/PrtSc** key combinations to get output on the printer (see Appendix G). Finally, type

PRINT N$

on a line by itself, followed by ® and observe what happens.

Now let's discover the effect of some BASIC "commands". First clear the screen with CLS, and then type LIST. Then type RENUM 100, followed by LIST. Finally, type NEW, followed by RUN and LIST. The program has disappeared.

1.2.2. Adding Two Numbers

The next program adds two numbers and prints their sum. Type NEW and then the following four lines:

```
10   INPUT A, B
20   SUM = A + B
30   PRINT "The answer is"; SUM
40   END
```

RUN the program, and the computer will display a "?", indicating that it is waiting for information (input) from you (the two numbers to be added). Type two numbers on the same line separated by a comma, so that the whole line looks like this:

? 2, 3®

Don't forget the ® or you will wait for ever! The answer (5 in this case) will be displayed on the screen. RUN the program a few more times using different data each time. Experiment with negative numbers and decimals.

The way in which the input data is presented is important. RUN the program again and try the following data:

? 2   3, 4®

Can you explain why the sum is given as 27? How about

? 2,®

as data (i.e. omitting the second number)?

Finally, if you give it only one number as data, with no final comma, as follows:

? 17®

it will respond with the phrase "Redo from start", meaning that you must re-enter all the data from scratch.

1.2.3. Compound Interest

Suppose you have $1000 in a savings account and want to calculate your new balance after interest at the rate of 4% has been added (compounded) to your account. It is very important in computer programming to have the problem sorted out in your own mind before you try to write the program. In this example, the logical breakdown, or "structure plan", of the problem is as follows:

1. Get data (initial balance and interest rate) into computer

2. Calculate interest (4% of $1000, i.e. $40)

3. Add interest to balance ($40 + $1000, i.e. $1040)

4. Print new balance.

A BASIC program to carry out this scheme is as follows:

```
10   A   = 1000
20   R   = 0.04
30   I   = A * R
```

```
40  A  = A + I
50  PRINT A
60  END
```

When you RUN the program, the answer of 1040 should be displayed. We will now discuss exactly what each line in the program means.

We need to distinguish immediately between two types of memory — PROGRAM memory, and ARITHMETIC memory — which are found in different places inside the computer.

The program memory, or workspace, holds the coded instructions of the program being executed, and consists of 65 529 different lines, each of which may contain BASIC instructions (statements). The lines in the workspace are numbered from 1 to 65 529. Each BASIC statement in the program must start with a number in this range, which indicates whereabouts in the workspace it will be placed. Thus after the above example has been typed in, line 30 in the workspace will contain the statement

I = A * R

("RUN" is not a BASIC statement, so it doesn't get a line number, and is consequently not stored in the workspace. It is a BASIC command which makes the computer carry out (execute) the statements in its workspace in ascending order of line number.) As long as all statements are correctly numbered, it doesn't matter in what order you type them; the computer sorts them into ascending order of line number. So if you type the statements in the order

```
50  PRINT A
20  R  = 0.04
30  I  = A * R
60  END
10  A  = 1000
40  A  = A + I
```

the workspace will look exactly the same as before. Clear the workspace with the command NEW and re-enter the program in a different order to verify this.

If two statements are given the same line number, then only the second one entered is kept in that line in the workspace; the previous statement is lost. A statement may be subsequently inserted between two statements already in the workspace by simply giving it an intermediate line number. It is thus customary to number the lines in 10s to start with so as to leave plenty of room for insertions.

The second type of memory, the arithmetic memory, holds all the numbers needed in the execution of the program, and may be thought of as a bank of boxes or cells, each of which can hold only one number. These boxes or cells are referred to by symbolic names in the BASIC statements. Thus the statement

```
10  A  = 1000
```

means "put the number 1000 into the box called A". Since the numbers in these boxes or cells may be changed by the program, they are called "variables", and we will usually refer to them as such. There are a vast number of possible names for these variables in BASIC: the general rule is that a variable name must begin with an alphabetic letter. The precise rules are spelled out in Chapter Two.

The statements in our compound interest program can now be interpreted as follows:

10 **Put the number 1000 into variable A;**
20 **Put the number 0.04 into variable R;**
30 **Multiply the number in A by the number in R and put the answer into variable I;**
40 **Add the number in A to the number in I and put the answer into variable A (what happens to the previous number in A?);**
50 **Print out the number in variable A;**
60 **There are no more statements in the program.**

When the program is RUN, all the variables in the arithmetic memory are set to zero initially. The program statements are then executed in order of line number. A snapshot of the arithmetic memory will then reveal the contents of A, I and R as follows:

A	1000/1040
I	40
R	0.04

All the other variables will be empty (have zero in them)

Note that the contents of variable A changes during execution of the program (this change is indicated by the "/" in the A box: the previous value of 1000 is lost). As an exercise enter the statement

10 A = 2000

(without removing the above program from the workspace), RUN the program, and make sure you understand what happens.

1.3. More Readable Programs and Output

Although the compound interest program works correctly it will be of limited value to anyone else since it doesn't say what it is trying to do or what the actual output of 1040 represents. There are two distinct ways of writing explanatory comments into your programs. They are discussed below. You should make full use of them.

1.3.1. The REM Statement

The general form of this BASIC statement is

n   REM whateveryouwouldliketo say

where n is a workspace line number. Whatever is typed after REM goes into the workspace at that line number, but is not executed. This enables you to put comments in your program to remind you (or anyone else who may be interested, like a lecturer trying to mark your program) what on earth is going on in the program.

1.3.2. Inline Comments

A comment may also be written after a BASIC statement on the same line if it is preceded by the single quote symbol. The computer ignores whatever follows it, but the comment is displayed when the workspace is listed. The general form is:

n   BASIC statement   'rhubarbrhubarb

where n is the line number.

1.3.3. A More Readable Example

Our compound interest program could be amended as follows:

```
 5   REM THIS PROGRAM COMPUTES COMPOUND INTEREST
10   A = 1000              'AMOUNT IN THE BANK
20   R = 0.04              'INTEREST RATE
30   I = A * R
40   A = A + I             'NEW BALANCE
50   PRINT "The new balance is:"; A
60   END
```

1.3.4. Re-arranging Output with PRINT

If line 50 is replaced by

50   PRINT I, A

two numbers, 40 and 1040, will be printed on the same line some distance apart. Try this out, and then try

50   PRINT I; A

to see what difference the semi-colon makes. Also try

50   PRINT I A

Next try the two lines

50   PRINT I,
55   PRINT A

and see if that makes any difference. Now remove line 55 and try

50   PRINT "The interest is"; I, "The new balance is"; A

Then see if the next two lines make any difference:

50   PRINT "The interest is"; I
55   PRINT "The new balance is"; A

Next try the three lines

50   PRINT I
52   PRINT
55   PRINT A

Finally try

50   PRINT TAB(10) A

The basic rules for the PRINT statement, which you may have discovered for yourself from the examples above, are as follows:

1. PRINT may include messages enclosed in double quotes, and/or variables (messages and variables will both be referred to as items).
2. A line of output is divided into print zones of 15 spaces each.
3. A comma after an item means that the next item will be printed in the next print zone, and on the same line (if there is room) even if its PRINT statement is further down the program.
4. A semi-colon after an item has the effect that only one or two spaces are left before printing the next item on the same line.
5. The absence of a comma or semi-colon after the last item in a PRINT statement means that the next item will be printed on a new line.
6. One or more spaces between two items in a PRINT have the same effect as a semi-colon.
7. TAB(n) may appear as a valid item in a PRINT statement, e.g.
   50   PRINT TAB(29) A
   will tabulate to column 29, i.e. printing of variable A will start in column 29.
8. LPRINT instead of PRINT causes the items in the statement to be printed on paper at the printer, instead of on the screen.
9. To promote good programming "style" (see next section) blanks should always be typed after commas and semi-colons in PRINT and LPRINT statements.
10. Hitting **Ctrl/PrtSc** before running a program causes all its output to go to the printer as well as to the screen. This continues to happen until **Ctrl/PrtSc** is hit again (it operates as a "toggle" switch).

1.3.5. Programming Style

Programs that are written any old how, while they may do what is required, can be difficult to follow when read again a month or two later. Throughout this book, therefore, attention will be paid to what is called programming style, by which is meant an emphasis on a neat and clear physical and logical layout of programs. Guidelines for good style are laid out in Appendix A.

1.4. Handling Program Files on Diskettes

Once a program is working correctly, you may wish to store it as a file on a diskette for future use. (A file is the general name for a collection of information on a diskette or tape.) The BASIC command

   SAVE "PROG"

for example, will save the current contents of the workspace on the diskette in drive A under the filename

   PROG.BAS

The three letter suffix .BAS is called an extension, and is always appended by the computer's operating system when a BASIC program is saved. Note that any previous version of the file PROG.BAS is lost once a new version is SAVEd. The SAVE command leaves the contents of the workspace intact. The command

   LOAD "PROG"

will copy the program stored on the diskette as PROG.BAS into the workspace, losing the previous contents of the workspace. The program on the diskette remains intact. It should be stressed that LOAD erases the current contents of the workspace before LOADing the requested program. Many a program has been lost by not paying attention to this detail. The BASIC command

    KILL "DUMMY.BAS"

will erase the diskette file DUMMY.BAS (note that the extension must be mentioned when KILLing). The command

    FILES

will list all the files on the diskette in drive A, while

    FILES "B:"

does the same for the diskette in drive B. The rules for writing filenames are as follows. A filename consists of two parts separated by a period, viz.

    name.extension

where the name may be from one to eight characters long, and the extension (automatically .BAS in the case of BASIC programs) from one to three. The following characters are allowed in the name and extension:

A to Z;
0 to 9;
( ) @ # $ % & ! − ' / ~

If your computer system has more than one disk drive and you want your programs stored, for example, on the diskette in drive B, you must prefix the filename with B:, e.g.

    SAVE "B:PROG"
    KILL "B:DUMMY.BAS"

It is wise to make frequent "backup" copies of all your important programs on a separate backup diskette, in case your master or working diskette becomes unreadable due to dirt, damage or decay. This can be done as follows. Once you have saved a program in the workspace on your master diskette, remove the master diskette from the drive, and insert the backup diskette. Repeat the SAVE command: the program in the workspace will now also be saved on the backup diskette. Alternatively, if you want to copy a program from your master diskette onto the backup diskette, LOAD the program from the master into the workspace, then replace the master with the backup, and SAVE the workspace on the backup diskette.

While entering a long program (i.e. more than 10 lines!) it is also wise to SAVE the workspace frequently (every 10 lines or so). You can use the same filename while doing this. This is a precaution against a power failure or some other disaster resulting in the irretrievable loss of the workspace.

1.5. BASIC Commands

It is important to distinguish between the effects of BASIC statements and commands. A statement is a line in a program which is only executed when the program is RUN, e.g.

40   A = A + 1

A command, however, has an immediate effect, e.g. RUN, LIST, etc. Some more important BASIC commands and their meanings are as follows (see Appendix C for a more comprehensive list):

AUTO n	Generate line numbers automatically starting from line n (if n is missing it is taken to be 10). This command is very useful when entering a long program. N.B. Before you use AUTO make sure you know how to get out of it (e.g. by pressing **Ctrl/Break** on the IBM PC).
CLS	Clear the screen.
DELETE n-m	Delete lines n to m inclusive (see Appendix C for all the possibilities).
LIST	List the entire workspace on the screen.
LIST n-m	List lines n to m inclusive (see Appendix C for all the possibilities).
LLIST	As for LIST, except that the lines are printed on the printer instead of the screen.
NEW	Clear the workspace and set all variables to zero.
RENUM	Renumber the entire workspace so that the new starting line number is 10 and the increment is 10 (see Appendix C for other possibilities).
RUN	Execute the program in the workspace.
RUN n	Execute from line n onwards.
RUN "PROG"	Load the program PROG from a diskette and run it.
SYSTEM	Exit from BASIC and return to the MSDOS Operating System.

These commands are also programmable, so that the statement

10 CLS

in a program will clear the screen when it is RUN. There is also the intriguing possibility of writing a program which destroys itself after executing!

REFERENCE

Galanter E. *Kids and Computers (The Parents' Microcomputer Handbook)*, Kingfisher Books, London, 1983.

1.6. EXERCISE

1.1 Write a BASIC program to compute and print the sum, difference, product and quotient of two numbers A and B (supplied by you). The symbol for division is the forward slash "/". Computers react differently to having to divide by zero. You can use this example to find out how the one you are using handles that problem.

2 ELEMENTARY BASIC

There are two essential requirements for successfully writing a computer program to solve a particular problem:

1. *THE EXACT RULES FOR CODING THE INSTRUCTIONS MUST BE LEARNT;*
2. *THE PROGRAMMER MUST DEVISE THE LOGIC NECESSARY FOR SOLVING THE PROBLEM (THIS CAN ONLY BE LEARNT BY PRACTICE).*

This chapter is devoted mainly to the first requirement: learning the coding rules. (A summary of all BASIC statements used in this book appears in Appendix B.)

2.1. Line Format

The general layout of a BASIC program line is:

n   BASIC statement   'comment

A statement may be continued on the next line if absolutely necessary, by typing past the end of the screen without pressing ® until the logical end of the statement is reached. This should be avoided wherever possible, as it makes for untidy programs. If a statement is too long for one line, it can often be broken up logically into smaller statements.

2.2. Arithmetic in BASIC

In this section we consider the basis of most computing: arithmetic.

2.2.1. Constants

A constant is any number that may be assigned to a variable, or used in a program. There are three main ways of expressing a constant: integer, fixed point, or floating point.

An integer is a whole number, without a decimal point, in the range -32768 to $+32767$. A fixed point constant is a number with a decimal point, e.g.

-7.654

A floating point constant is a number with two parts, the mantissa and the exponent, separated by an E. The mantissa is multiplied by the power of 10 indicated by the exponent. The mantissa may be an integer or fixed point constant, but the exponent must be an integer (signed or unsigned). E.g.

    1.23E−4   (= 0.000123)
    123E2   (= 12300)

A floating point constant may be in the range $2.9E-39$ to $1.7E+38$ (positive or negative). Note that a decimal point is used, not a comma!

2.2.2. Variables

A variable is the name used to represent values in the arithmetic memory. In Microsoft BASIC a variable name may be of any length, although if it is longer than 40 characters, only the first 40 characters are significant (other versions of BASIC are usually more restrictive in the way that variables may be named).

The characters allowed in a variable name are letters and numbers, and the decimal point, but the first character must be a letter. There are exceptions to this rule as we shall see below.

A variable name may not be a "reserved word". These have a special meaning in BASIC, like PRINT, END, etc. There is a list of reserved words in Appendix D. Reserved words may, however, be embedded in variable names, like NEWTON (the reserved word being the command NEW), although they may not have type declaration characters appended (see below).

The following are examples of valid and invalid variable names:

Valid variable name	Invalid variable name (why?)
X	2A
R2D2	$5
ENDOFTHEMONTH	HP41−C
RUN.1	LIST

Variables are divided into different types. By default, all variables are of type "single precision", which means that they need four bytes (32 bits) of storage to represent them. A bit is the basic unit of information in a digital computer, and is a contraction of "**BI**nary digi**T**". The two binary digits are 0 and 1. Single precision gives an accuracy of six digits, although seven are printed for some obscure reason (the last digit is garbage).

The % type declaration character at the end of a variable name specifies it with type integer, which only needs two bytes (16 bits) of storage. The DEFINT statement may also be used to declare all variables beginning with certain letters as integers. E.g. the statement

10 DEFINT B, I-N

will specify all variables with initial letters B and I to N inclusive with type integer.

This declaration is a "non-executable" statement, and should appear at the start of a program, before the first executable statement (an executable statement is one that does something, like INPUT).

Since arithmetic is much faster using integer variables as opposed to single precision ones, it makes good sense to declare all variables integer that do not actually require decimal parts.

The type declaration character for single precision is the exclamation mark (e.g. MONEY!), although this is seldom used since all variables are single precision by default.

To promote good programming style, it is recommended that every variable used in a program be described in a REM statement, at the start of the program, in alphabetical order. Many of the examples in this book follow this practice, although not always, in order to save paper.

2.2.3. Example: Vertical Motion under Gravity

Using simple dynamical laws, one can show that if a stone is projected vertically upward with an initial speed u, its vertical displacement s after a time t has elapsed is given by the formula

$$s = ut - 0.5gt^2,$$

where $g = 9.8$ metres/sec^2, the acceleration due to gravity. Air resistance has been ignored. We would like to compute s, given u and t. Notice that we are not concerned here with how to derive the formula, but how to compute its value. The structure plan of the problem is very simple:

1. Get values of g, u, and t into the computer;
2. Compute the value of s according to the formula;
3. Print the value of s.

```
100   REM VERTICAL MOTION UNDER GRAVITY
110                                          '
120   REM G: ACCELERATION DUE TO GRAVITY
130   REM S: DISPLACEMENT IN METRES
140   REM T: TIME IN SECONDS
150   REM U: INITIAL SPEED IN M/S
160                                          '
170   CLS                        'CLEARS THE SCREEN
180   G = 9.8
190   U = 60
200   T = 6
210   S = U * T - G / 2 * T^2
220   PRINT "TIME", "DISPLACEMENT"
230   PRINT
240   PRINT T, S
990   END
```

Run this example as an exercise. It is discussed further in the Exercises at the end of the chapter.

2.2.4. Assignment Statements

This is a way of assigning a value to a variable. The most general form of the assignment statement is

n   variable = formula

where the formula (or "expression") on the RHS is constructed from variables and constants using the basic arithmetic operations of addition, subtraction, multiplication, division and exponentiation (raise to the power of). The symbols for these operations, and examples of their use are given in the next section.

If the variable is of integer type, the value assigned to it is rounded up (i.e. 2.5 becomes 3, whereas 2.49 becomes 2). E.g. the program segment

```
10   I% = 1.499
20   J% = 2 / 3
```

will assign the value 1 to both I% and J%.

2.2.5. Arithmetic Operators

The arithmetic operators, in order of precedence, are as follows:

Operator	Operation	Example of use
^	Exponentiation	X ^ 3 (X * X * X)
−	Negation	− X
* and /	Multiplication and floating point division	A * B A / B
\	Integer division	A \ B
MOD	Modulo arithmetic	X MOD Y
+ and −	Addition and subtraction	A + B A − B

Of these operations, the integer division and modulo arithmetic may require some explanation.

In integer division the operands are rounded to integers before the division is performed, and the quotient is truncated to an integer (i.e. the decimal part is chopped off, not rounded). The following program segment illustrates integer division:

```
10  A = 10 \ 3
20  B = 27.88 \ 7.49
30  PRINT A; B
RUN
 3    4
```

The effect of the MOD operator is to compute the integer remainder when the first operand is divided by the second, after both operands have been rounded to integers. E.g.

```
10  A = 10 MOD 3
20  B = 27.88 MOD 7.49
30  PRINT A; B
RUN
 1    0
```

The first result occurs because 3 goes 3 times into 10 with a remainder of 1. In line 20 the operands are rounded to 28 and 7, and since 7 divides exactly 4 times into 28, there is no remainder.

To promote good programming style, it is recommended that blanks always be typed on either side of operators.

2.2.6. Precedence of Operations

Ambiguities can arise in the evaluation of expressions, e.g. does A/B*3 mean A/(B*3) or (A/B)*3? To avoid such problems, expressions are evaluated in a program according to strict rules of precedence. Parentheses (brackets) have the highest precedence, so that calculations within the innermost parentheses of an expression are carried out first. Precedence for the remaining operations are as set out in §2.2.5. If two operations with the same precedence, like multiplication and division, occur in the same expression, BASIC evaluates them from left to right. So A/B*3 is in fact evaluated as (A/B)*3.

2.3. The INPUT Statement

In the compound interest program in Chapter One the data for the program was supplied using the assignment statements

```
10   A = 1000
20   R = 0.04
```

This is a rather inflexible way of supplying data, since to run the program for different amounts or interest rates, you would have to change these statements, and there may be many such assignment statements in a more complicated program. The INPUT statement, however, which we also saw in Chapter One, allows you to supply the data while the program is executing, rather than before execution, as in the case of the assignment statement. The general form is

n   INPUT [;] ["Prompt";] list of variables separated by commas

The actual values to be given to the variables must be typed on one line following the RUN command. The compound interest problem could be rewritten as follows:

```
10   INPUT A, R
20   I  = A * R
30   A  = A + I
40   PRINT "The new balance is"; A
50   END
RUN
? 1000, 0.04
The new balance is 1040
```

To re-run with different data, run the program again and type the new data on the same line as the question mark. Whenever BASIC encounters the INPUT statement it displays the question mark prompt to indicate that it is waiting for data.

Note:

1. Values for INPUT must be separated by commas. Blanks are ignored by INPUT, unless the entire number is blank, in which case it is taken to be zero. E.g. if your response is

    ? 1000 0.04,

    the effect is to assign the value 10000.04 to A and 0 to R.

2. If too few or too many items are typed in response to INPUT, the message

    ?Redo from start

    is displayed, and all the data for that INPUT must be entered again.

3. There may be separate INPUT statements for A and R. But then the data must be on separate lines too:

```
10   INPUT A
15   INPUT R
.....
RUN
? 1000
? 0.04
```

4. If a prompt is typed in the INPUT statement, it is displayed before the question mark, e.g.

   ```
   10   INPUT "INTEREST RATE"; R
   RUN
   INTEREST RATE? ©
   ```

   where the © symbol indicates the position of the cursor on the screen.

5. If the semi-colon after the prompt is replaced by a comma, the question mark is suppressed:

   ```
   10   INPUT "AMOUNT:", A
   RUN
   AMOUNT: ©
   ```

6. If the optional semi-colon immediately after the word INPUT is used the cursor remains on the same line as the data after ® is pressed.

2.3.1. *Example: Future Value of an Investment*

If an amount of money A is invested for k years at a nominal annual interest rate r, the value V of the investment after k years is given by

$$V = A(1 + r/n)^{nk}$$

where n is the number of compounding periods per year. The following program computes the value of this formula for any input.

```
100   REM FUTURE VALUE OF AN INVESTMENT
110   '
120   INPUT "INITIAL AMOUNT:", A
130   INPUT "ANNUAL INTEREST RATE (PERCENT):", R
140   INPUT "COMPOUNDING PERIODS PER YEAR:", N
150   INPUT "NUMBER OF YEARS:", K
160   '
170   R = R / 100                 'CONVERT TO DECIMAL FRACTION
180   VALUE = A * (1 + R / N) ^ (N * K)
190   PRINT
200   PRINT "FINAL VALUE:"; VALUE
210   END
RUN
INITIAL AMOUNT: 1000
ANNUAL INTEREST RATE (PERCENT): 4
COMPOUNDING PERIODS PER YEAR: 1
NUMBER OF YEARS: 10

FINAL VALUE:    1480.244
```

2.4. Repeating with FOR-NEXT: Compound Interest

In this section we introduce two very powerful BASIC constructions: FOR-NEXT, and IF-THEN-ELSE.

Suppose we have four different savings accounts, with balances of $1000, $500, $758 and $12750 respectively, and want to compute the new balance in each of them after 4% interest has been compounded. This could be done using a FOR-NEXT loop with a counter:

```
10   R = 0.04
20   FOR I = 1 TO 4
30     INPUT; "OLD BALANCE: ", A
40     B = A + A * R
50     PRINT TAB(24) "NEW BALANCE:"; B
60   NEXT I
70   END
RUN
OLD BALANCE: 1000      NEW BALANCE: 1040
OLD BALANCE: 500       NEW BALANCE: 520
OLD BALANCE: 758       NEW BALANCE: 788.32
OLD BALANCE: 12750     NEW BALANCE: 13260
```

Run this as an exercise. The four amounts are entered in response to the prompt "OLD BALANCE:". Note the use of the semi-colon in line 30 to get the output on the same line as the input.

The general structure of the FOR-NEXT loop is as follows:

```
n    FOR I = J TO K
       ....
       ....
m    NEXT I
```

where I is any BASIC variable (preferably of type integer), J and K may be constants or BASIC variables or expressions, and n and m are line numbers. All the statements between FOR and NEXT will be repeatedly executed. The numerical values of J and K determine how many repeats are made. On the the first loop, I is given the value J, and is then increased by one at the end of each loop. Looping stops once I has reached the value K.

Most banks and building societies offer differential interest rates. Suppose in the above example that the interest is still 4% for balances less than $5000, but 10% otherwise. We could amend the program to allow for this by deleting line 10 and inserting a new line 35 as follows:

```
20   FOR I = 1 TO 4
30     INPUT; "OLD BALANCE: ", A
35     IF A >= 5000 THEN R = 0.1 ELSE R = 0.04
40     B = A + A * R
50     ....
```

Try this out to verify that it has the intended effect. We will consider the IF-THEN-ELSE statement more fully later in the chapter.

As a variation on our compound interest problem, suppose we want to work out, from first principles (i.e. without using the formula quoted in §2.3.1), the new balance in a particular account after, say, 10 years of compounding at the same rate of 4% p.a. We could build up the solution step by step ourselves. If the initial balance is $1000, after one year the balance is $1040 as we have already seen. After another year (assuming no further deposits) the new balance is

$1040 + 4\%$ of $1040 = $1081.60.

Continuing like this, the balance after three years is $1124.86. After ten years, it is $1480.24. To compute this, we must execute not once, but ten times, the part of the program that compounds the interest, i.e. the statement

230   AMT = AMT + RATE * AMT

in the program below (it will also be useful to print out the new balance every year). This may also easily be done using a FOR-NEXT loop with a counter:

```
100   REM COMPOUNDS INTEREST ANNUALLY OVER 10 YEARS
110   '
120   REM AMT : AMOUNT IN ACCOUNT
130   REM RATE : ANNUAL INTEREST RATE
140   REM YR   : YEAR
150   '
160   INPUT AMT, RATE
170   CLS                     'CLEAR THE SCREEN
180   PRINT "INTEREST ON"; AMT; "AT"; 100 * RATE; "%"
190   PRINT
200   PRINT "YEAR", "BALANCE"
210   PRINT
220   FOR YR = 1985 TO 1994
230      AMT = AMT + RATE * AMT
240      PRINT YR, AMT
250   NEXT YR
990   END
RUN
```

INTEREST ON 1000 AT 4 %

YEAR	BALANCE
1985	1040
1986	1081.6
1987	1124.864
1988	1169.859
1989	1216.653
1990	1265.319
1991	1315.932
1992	1368.569
1993	1423.312
1994	1480.244

If you want to find out how to restrict the number of decimal places in the output, you can read up about the PRINT USING statement in Chapter Eight.

There is more about the FOR-NEXT statement in Chapter Five.

2.5. Example: Final Course Mark

The year mark, or class record, of a class of students taking a certain course is calculated as follows. During the year they write two tests (each out of 25 marks), and have to do some computing projects (out of 50 marks altogether). At the end of the year they write a final examination (out of 100 marks). The first test counts 20% towards the class record, the second counts 30%, and the computing counts 50%. The class record is counted toward their final mark only if it exceeds the examination mark, in which case it counts 25% toward the final mark, the exam mark counting 75%.

The following program computes and prints each student's year mark and final course mark and whether the student passes or fails (50% being the pass mark). The data for each student is entered in a DATA statement whence it gets into the arithmetic memory via the READ statement when the program is run, instead of via INPUT. The READ-DATA statements are discussed in more detail below in §2.7. READ-DATA is extremely useful when developing a program that requires a fair amount of test data, since the data does not have to be entered all over again each time the program is run.

```
100  REM FINAL COURSE MARK BASED ON CLASS RECORD AND EXAM
110       '
120  REM COMP       COMPUTING MARK
130  REM CRM        CLASS RECORD MARK
140  REM EXM        EXAM MARK
150  REM FIN        FINAL COURSE MARK
160  REM STU%       STUDENT COUNTER
170  REM T1         FIRST TEST MARK
180  REM T2         SECOND TEST MARK
190       '
200  CLS
210  PRINT "CLASS RECORD", "EXAM", "FINAL MARK"
220  PRINT
230       '
240  FOR STU% = 1 TO 60
250     READ T1, T2, COMP, EXM
260     CRM = T1 / 25 * 20 + T2 / 25 * 30 + COMP
270     IF EXM >= CRM THEN FIN = EXM ELSE FIN = .25 * CRM + .75 * EXM
280     PRINT CRM, EXM, FIN,
290     IF FIN >= 50 THEN PRINT "PASS" ELSE PRINT "FAIL"
300  NEXT STU%
310       '
320  DATA 15, 20, 35, 57
330  DATA 1, 2, 3, 50                    exactly 60 lines of data
340  DATA 0, 24, 23, 7
350  ....
...
990  END
```

Run this example with sample data for a class of, say, five students. Note that the last comma in line 280 ensures that the comment "PASS" or "FAIL" is printed on the same line as the relevant marks.

2.6. Deciding with IF-THEN-ELSE

In the above example we see a situation where the computer must make decisions

— whether or not to include the class record, and whether to print "PASS" or "FAIL". In fact, the programmer cannot be sure which of these possibilities will occur when writing the program, so the program must be designed to allow for all of them. We need a conditional branch instruction, the most general form of which is

n   IF condition THEN s1 [ELSE s2]

or

n   IF expression relational operator expression THEN s1 [ELSE s2]

where "expression" stands for any BASIC variable or formula, and s1 and s2 are any BASIC statements. If the condition is true, s1 is executed, otherwise s2 is executed. The ELSE part of the statement is optional, and may be left out, so that in the student mark program, line 290 could be replaced by

```
290   IF FIN >= 50 THEN PRINT "PASS"
295   IF FIN < 50 THEN PRINT "FAIL"
```

There are six relational operators that may be used in forming the condition in an IF-THEN-ELSE:

Relational Operator	Meaning
<	is less than
>	is greater than
=	is equal to
<> or ><	is not equal to
<= or =<	is less than or equal to
>= or =>	is greater than or equal to

For example

n   IF B * B − 4 * A * C < 0 THEN PRINT "ROOTS ARE IMAGINARY"

The condition in the IF-THEN-ELSE may be constructed from other conditions using the logical operators OR, AND and NOT. For example, suppose we wanted to print out the class (grade) of each student's final course mark in the above program. Then we would need to replace line 290 by the following:

```
282   IF FIN >= 75 THEN PRINT "I"
284   IF FIN >= 70 AND FIN < 75 THEN PRINT "II+"
286   IF FIN >= 60 AND FIN < 70 THEN PRINT "II−"
288   IF FIN >= 50 AND FIN < 60 THEN PRINT "III"
290   IF FIN < 50 THEN PRINT "FAIL"
```

The PRINT in each statement is executed only if both conditions are true. But in something like

n   IF A < 0 OR A > 0 THEN ROOT = − B / (2 * A)

the statement following THEN is executed if either (or both) of the conditions A < 0 or A > 0 is true. Incidentally, this statement is equivalent to either of the following:

n   IF NOT A = 0 THEN ROOT = − B / (2 * A)

n   IF A <> 0 THEN ROOT = − B / (2 * A)

Example: Input two numbers and print out whether they are equal, and if not, print out the larger one.

```
10   INPUT X, Y
20   IF X = Y THEN PRINT "NUMBERS EQUAL"
30   IF X > Y THEN PRINT X; "IS LARGER"
40   IF X < Y THEN PRINT Y; "IS LARGER"
```

The logical operators are defined by the following "truth table" (in order of precedence). "r" and "s" stand for "logical expressions", like

FIN >= 70

In Microsoft BASIC "true" is represented by the value -1, and "false" by 0.

r	s	NOT r	r AND s	r OR s	r XOR s	r EQV s	r IMP s
T	T	F	T	T	F	T	T
T	F	F	F	T	T	F	F
F	T	T	F	T	T	F	T
F	F	T	F	F	F	T	T

2.7. The READ-DATA Statements

This is the third way of assigning values to variables. It is less flexible than INPUT, but is better to use when large volumes of data are involved, or when the programmer is not sure how many numbers will appear in each DATA statement. The general form of the statements is

n   READ (variables, separated by commas)
m   DATA (values for the variables, separated by commas)

Example:

```
10   READ X, Y
20   DATA −1, 2
30   PRINT X; Y
RUN
−1   2
```

Note:

1. There must be a DATA value for each variable listed in a READ statement. If there are not enough, the program "crashes" with an "Out of data" message.

2. During execution of READs the computer searches the entire program for DATA statements until all the variables have been assigned values. The DATA statements may therefore be placed anywhere in the program.

3. Additional values in a DATA statement are not ignored, and will be used by subsequent READs, e.g.

```
 10  DATA 7, 13, −5
 20  READ A, B
 30  READ C, D
 40  DATA 17
 50  PRINT A; B; C; D
RUN
  7  13 −5  17
```

4. A DATA statement may not have an inline comment.

2.8. String Variables

One glaring problem with our student mark program in §2.5 is that the students' names are not printed out! To remedy this, we introduce the concept of a string variable, which is the third type of variable we have seen so far, the other types being integer and single precision. A string variable is able to hold a string of characters instead of a numeric value. A $ type declaration character at the end of a variable name specifies it with type string. The DEFSTR declaration may also be used at the start of a program to declare all variables starting with the given letter(s) as string variables.

2.8.1. Assignment of Strings

A string of characters may be placed in a string variable as follows:

```
10  DAT$ = "21"
20  SUFF$ = "st"
30  PRINT DAT$; SUFF$
RUN
21st
```

2.8.2. Strings as Data

The program in §2.5 may be amended to allow for student names by typing the names in the DATA statements, and making some other changes. The following line should be added to the program:

```
155  REM NAM$ : STUDENT'S NAME
```

and the following lines need to be changed:

```
210  PRINT "NAME", "CLASS RECORD", "EXAM", "FINAL MARK"
250    READ NAM$, T1, T2, COMP, EXM
280    PRINT NAM$, CRM, EXM, FIN,
320  DATA BAKER A.B., 15, 20, 35, 57
330  DATA JONES R.Q., 1, 2, 3, 50
340  DATA SMITH X.Z., 0, 24, 23, 7
... etc.
```

If this program is run for a sample class of three students, the output is as follows:

NAME	CLASS RECORD	EXAM	FINAL MARK	
BAKER A.B.	71	57	60.5	PASS
JONES R.Q.	6.2	50	50	PASS
SMITH X.Z.	51.8	7	18.2	FAIL

Note:

1. A comma signals the end of an item in a DATA statement. So the statement

    320   DATA BAKER, A.B., 15, 20, 35, 57

    in the above example will cause an error. The string "BAKER" will be assigned to NAM$. The program will then attempt to put "A.B." into T1, but will fail because T1 is not a string variable.

2. Embedded blanks are not ignored in strings, since the blank itself is a valid character.

3. If string variable names are separated by a semi-colon in a PRINT statement, they will be printed without blanks between them on the same line, e.g.

    ```
    40   N$ = "$"
    50   R$ = "10.00"
    60   PRINT N$; R$
    RUN
    $10.00
    ```

4. Strings may or may not be enclosed in quotes in a DATA statement, but if quotes are not used, leading and trailing blanks are ignored. Commas may appear as valid characters in a string as long as the whole string is enclosed in quotes. E.g. the program segment

    ```
    10   READ D$
    20   DATA "NOVEMBER, 1946", 21
    30   READ D
    40   PRINT D; D$
    ```

    will result in the output

    21 NOVEMBER, 1946

    but if the quotes are removed from line 20, the output will be

    1946 NOVEMBER

    and the number 21 will be read into the next numeric variable appearing in the next READ statement to occur in the program (which may not be what you intended!).

5. INPUT works the same way with strings as READ-DATA. The string need only be enclosed in quotes if it has commas or leading and trailing blanks which should not be discarded.

2.8.3. Concatenation of Strings

String variables (or constants) may be concatenated (joined) with the addition operator, as follows:

```
10   N$ = "TWEEDLED"
20   UM$ = "UM"
30   EE$ = "EE"
40   T.1$ = N$ + UM$
50   T.2$ = N$ + EE$
60   PRINT T.1$
```

```
70 PRINT T.2$
RUN
TWEEDLEDUM
TWEEDLEDEE
```

This can be useful, for example, when handling output files with more than one disk drive (see §8.4.1).

2.9. EXERCISES

2.1 Evaluate the following formulae given that
A = 2, B = 3, C = 4:

X = A / 2 * B	(3, not 1/3)
X = A / B ^ 2	(2/9)
X = (A / B) ^ 2	(4/9)
X = A + B * C − 4	(10)
X = A ^ 2 * B / C + 3	(6)
X = A ^ (2 * B) / (C + 3)	(64/7)
X = A * B + C	(10)
X = 9.5 MOD 3.2	(1)
X = 2.56 \ 1.28	(3)

2.2 Decide which of the following constants are not written in acceptable Microsoft BASIC and state why not:

(a) 9,87　　(b) .0　　(c) 25.82　　(d) −356231
(e) 3.57 * E2　　(f) 3.57E2　　(g) 3.57E+2　　(h) 3,57E−2

2.3 State, giving reasons, which of the following are not acceptable Microsoft BASIC variable names:

(a) A2　　(b) A.2　　(c) 2A　　(d) 'A' ONE
(e) BASIC　　(f) MIN*2　　(g) ALPHONE　　(h) INT+1
(i) BINGO　　(j) NAME$　　(k) VARPTR$　　(l) MK%

2.4 Translate the following arithmetic expressions into BASIC expressions:

(a) $p + \dfrac{w}{u}$　　(b) $p = \dfrac{w}{u+v}$　　(c) $\dfrac{p + \dfrac{w}{u+v}}{p + \dfrac{w}{u-v}}$　　(d) x^2

(e) $x^{2.5}$　　(f) $x^{\frac{1}{2}}$　　(g) x^{y+z}　　(h) $(x^y)^z$

(i) $x^{(y^z)}$　　(j) $x - \dfrac{x^3}{3!} + \dfrac{x^5}{5!}$　　(k) $\dfrac{-b + (b^2 - 4ac)^{\frac{1}{2}}}{2a}$

2.5 Translate the following into BASIC statements:
　(a) Add one to the value of I and store it in I.
　(b) Cube I, add J to this, and store the result in I.
　(c) Set G equal to the larger of the two values E and F.

(d) If D is greater than zero, set X equal to minus B.
(e) If I is even, set X equal to minus X.
(f) Find the remainder when I is divided by J and store it in K (assume that I and J are integers).

2.6 This question refers to the vertical motion example of §2.2.
  (a) Run the program as it stands. Can you work out whether the stone is moving up or down?
  (b) Rerun for different values of *t*. In particular, use the program to find out where the stone is after 20 seconds, and interpret your results physically.
  (c) Re-arrange the formula in order to compute when the stone returns to the ground.
  (d) Re-arrange the formula in order to compute when the stone is at any particular height, i.e. compute *t*, given *u* and *s*. Interpret your results physically.

2.7 Write a program which will convert a temperature on the Fahrenheit scale (where water freezes and boils at 32° and 212° respectively) to the more familiar Centigrade scale. The logical analysis, or structure plan, is as follows:

  1. Get Fahrenheit temperature into computer (call it TEMPF)
  2. Work out its Centigrade equivalent (call it TEMPC)
     2.1. Subtract 32 from TEMPF and multiply by 5/9
  3. Print the value of TEMPC.

2.8 Write a program which converts a temperature on the Centigrade scale to one on the Fahrenheit scale.

2.9 Try to work out the output of the following program before checking your answers on the computer:

```
10  READ X, Y
20  READ N$, M$
30  DATA 1.2
40  DATA 3, PLONK, "JONES, I."
50  PRINT X;Y; N$; M$
```

2.10 Write some lines of BASIC which will exchange the contents of two memory variables A and B, using only one additional memory variable T.

2.11 Write some lines of BASIC which will exchange the contents of two memory variables, without using any additional variables.

2.12 What are the values of A and X after the following program has been executed?

```
110  A = 0
120  I = 1
130  X = 0
140  A = A + I
150  X = X + I / A
160  A = A + I
170  X = X + I / A
180  A = A + I
190  X = X + I / A
200  A = A + I
210  X = X + I / A
```

2.13 Rewrite the program in Ex. 2.12 more economically by using a FOR-NEXT loop.

2.14 Work out by hand the output of the following program. What does it do in general?

```
10  N = 4
20  S = 0
30  FOR K = 1 TO N
40    S = S + 1 / (K * K)
50  NEXT K
60  PRINT (6 * S) ^ 0.5
70  END
```

If you run this program for larger and larger values of N you will find that the output approaches a well known limit.

2.15 Try to spot the syntax errors (see Chapter Seven) in this program before running it on the computer to check your answers with the error messages generated by the computer:

```
10  READ A, B
20  C+1 = A
30  B = (A + 1)(C + 2)
40  D = (A + (B / 2A )
50  PRINT 'THE ANSWER IS': A; B
60  END.
```

2.16 A student makes a regular deposit of $20 each month into his bank account. Interest is compounded at the end of each month, after the deposit has been made, at the rate of 1.5% per month. He starts with nothing in the account. Write a program which prints out, under suitable headings, the interest and month end balance each month for two years. Use first principles, i.e. do not make use of the formula quoted in Ex. 2.17.

2.17 The future value (or annuity) of a regular fixed deposit D which is made n times a year for k years, where the nominal rate is r, is given by the formula

$D[(1 + r/n)^{nk} - 1] / (r/n)$.

Write a program which input values of D, r, n and k and prints out the future value.

2.18 The regular fixed payments P, made n times per year, to repay a loan of amount A over a period of k years, where the nominal annual interest rate is r, are given by

$P = (r/n)A(1 + r/n)^{nk} / [(1 + r/n)^{nk} - 1]$.

Write a program to compute P for any input. (This formula is used in §12.2.2 to obtain a graphical display of the outstanding balance of the loan against time.)

3 PROGRAM PREPARATION

Our examples so far have been very simple logically, since we have been concentrating on the technical aspects of writing BASIC statements correctly. However, real problems are far more complex, and to program successfully we need to understand the problem thoroughly, and to break it down into its most fundamental logical stages. In other words, we have to develop a systematic procedure, or "algorithm", for solving the problem. There are a number of ways which assist in this process of algorithm development. In this chapter we outline two such methods: flowcharts, and structure plans (Ellis, 1982). Both approaches are used here, and it is up to you to decide which you prefer.

3.1. Flowcharting Symbols

The compound interest problem in §1.2.3 can be represented logically as follows (the symbols are explained below):

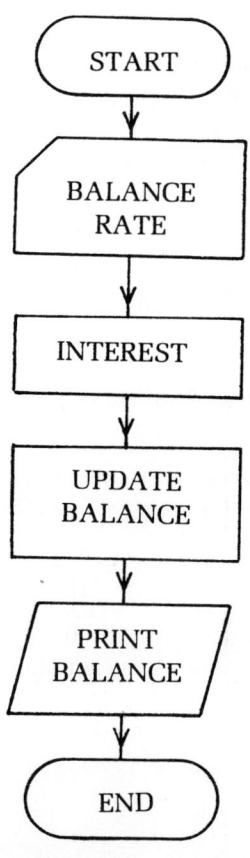

The main symbols used in flowcharts, and their meanings, are:

———→——— flow of logic

  Start/End

  Input (or assignment) of information

  Processing (e.g. calculation of formulae)

  Decision (two-way branch)

  Header for loop structure

  End of loop

  Printed output

3.2. Student Mark Problem

Using these symbols, the student mark problem of Chapter Two can be represented logically as follows (notice that the boxes do not necessarily contain details of the calculations):

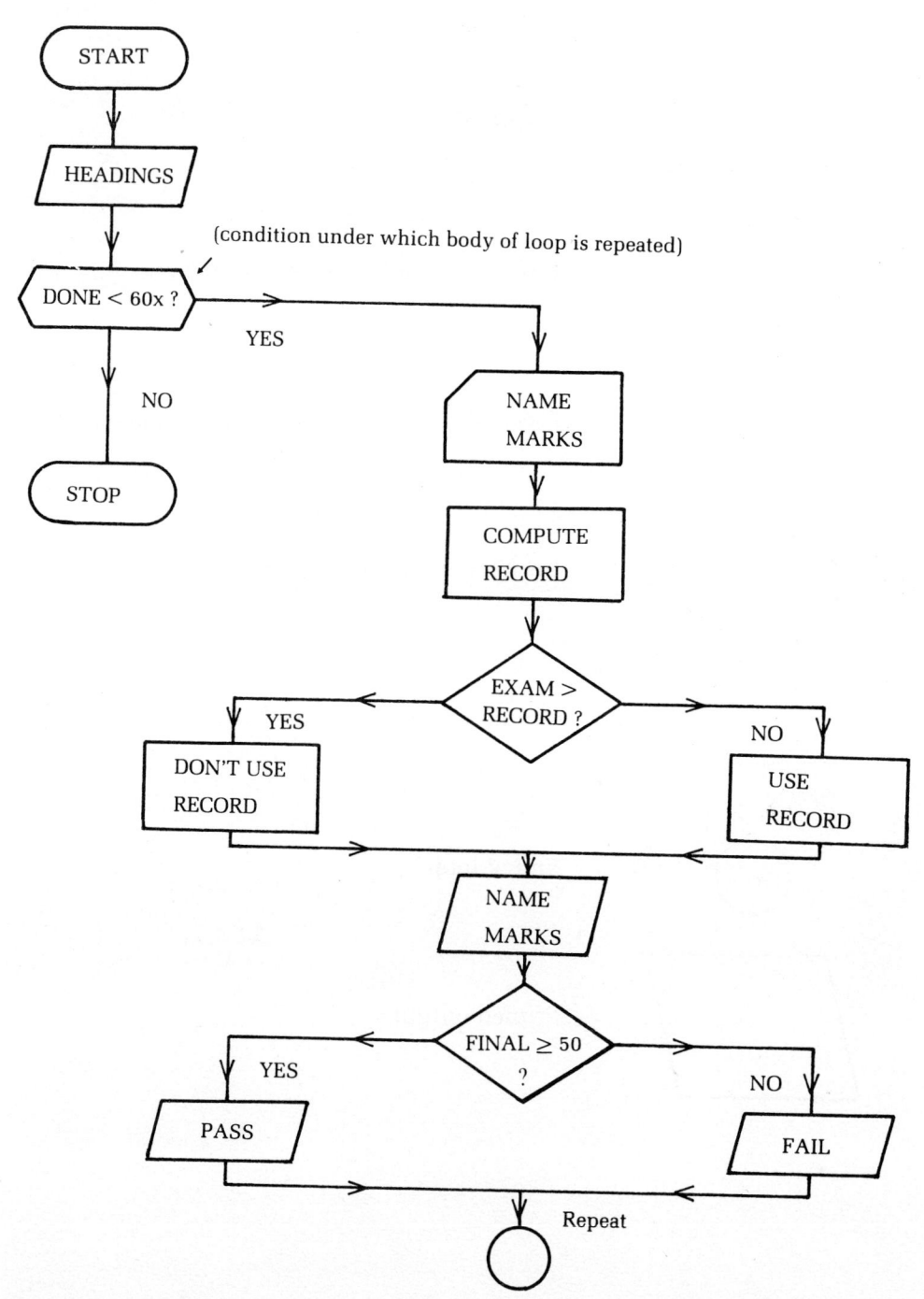

```
                    START
                      │
                      ▼
                  ┌─────────┐
                  │HEADINGS │
                  └─────────┘
                      │      (condition under which body of loop is repeated)
                      ▼     ↙
                  ╱DONE<60x?╲─────────────────────────┐
                  ╲         ╱       YES               │
                      │                               ▼
                      │ NO                        ╱NAME  ╱
                      ▼                          ╱MARKS ╱
                    STOP                            │
                                                    ▼
                                             ┌──────────┐
                                             │ COMPUTE  │
                                             │ RECORD   │
                                             └──────────┘
                                                    │
                                                    ▼
                        ┌──────────────── ╱EXAM >  ╲ ────────────────┐
                        │     YES          ╲RECORD?╱       NO        │
                        ▼                                             ▼
                  ┌──────────┐                                 ┌──────────┐
                  │DON'T USE │                                 │   USE    │
                  │ RECORD   │                                 │ RECORD   │
                  └──────────┘                                 └──────────┘
                        │                                             │
                        └─────────────────┬───────────────────────────┘
                                          ▼
                                      ╱ NAME  ╱
                                     ╱ MARKS ╱
                                          │
                                          ▼
                        ┌──────────── ╱FINAL ≥ 50╲ ────────────┐
                        │    YES       ╲   ?    ╱      NO      │
                        ▼                                       ▼
                     ╱PASS╱                                  ╱FAIL╱
                        │                                       │
                        └───────────────┬───────────────────────┘
                                        ▼
                                     Repeat
                                       ◯
```

3.3. Company Payroll

A company has two categories of sales personnel. Senior salesmen receive a salary of $1000 a month plus a 5% commission on their monthly sales, while juniors get $750 a month plus 3% of their sales. As chief accountant you are required to write a program that will print out each salesman's name, rank (i.e. "Senior" or "Junior"), monthly sales, and monthly pay. Finally it must print out the total number of people on the payroll, and the total monthly salary bill. For each employee there is to be a DATA statement in the program with his name, his monthly sales, and a pay code (1 for senior; 2 for junior). The employees' data are preceeded by a DATA statement containing the total number of employees.

With a more complex problem like this, it is almost essential to draw a flowchart of the logic before attempting to write the program. The flowchart follows below, but the program is in the next chapter, because the best way to handle a problem like this is to use the subroutine structure, GOSUB-RETURN, which is introduced there.

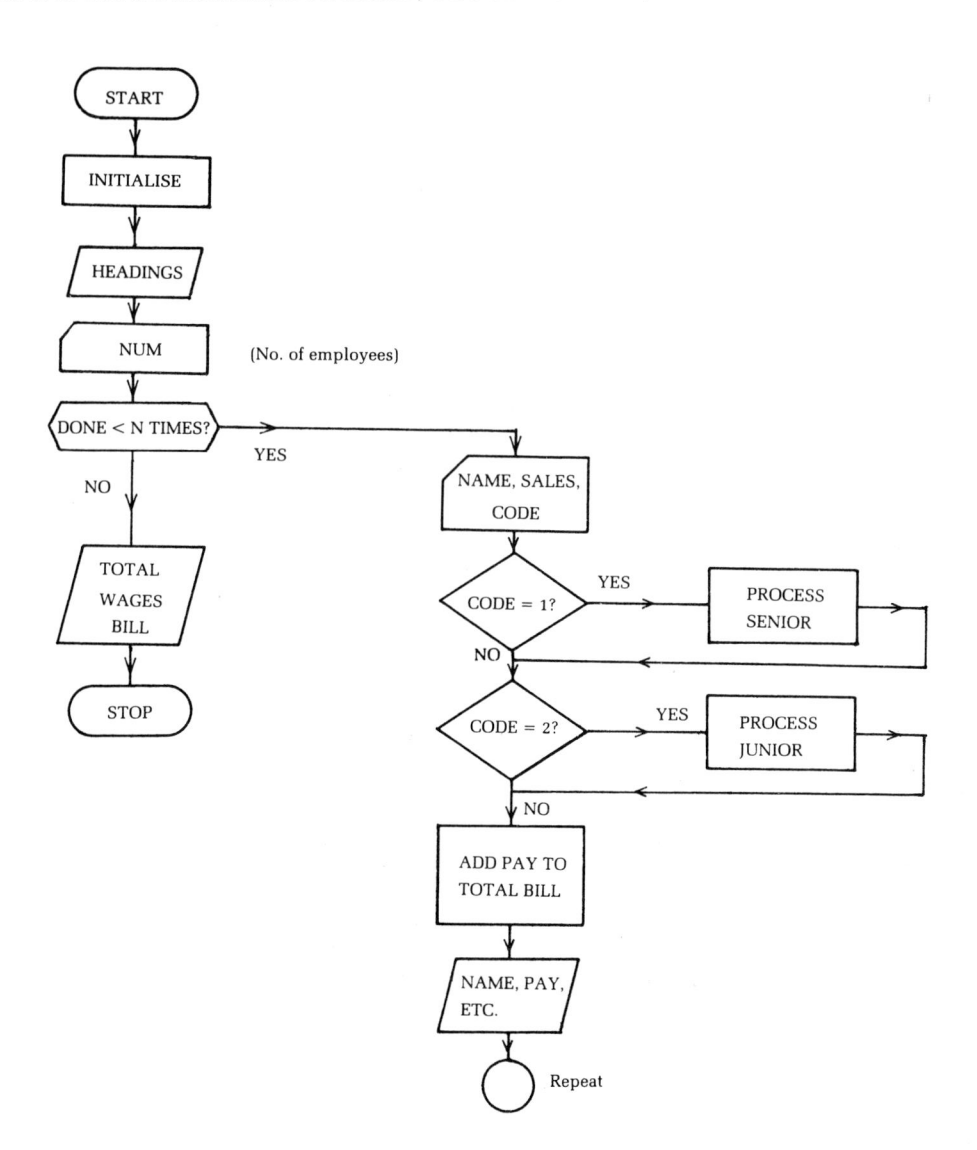

3.4. Largest Number in a List

After a class test, suppose that each student's name is typed in a DATA stastement, followed by his/her mark for the test (assume all marks are at least zero). There are exactly 50 students in the class. Write a program which prints out the name of the student with the highest mark, together with the mark. The flowchart is as follows, but again, the program must wait until the next chapter.

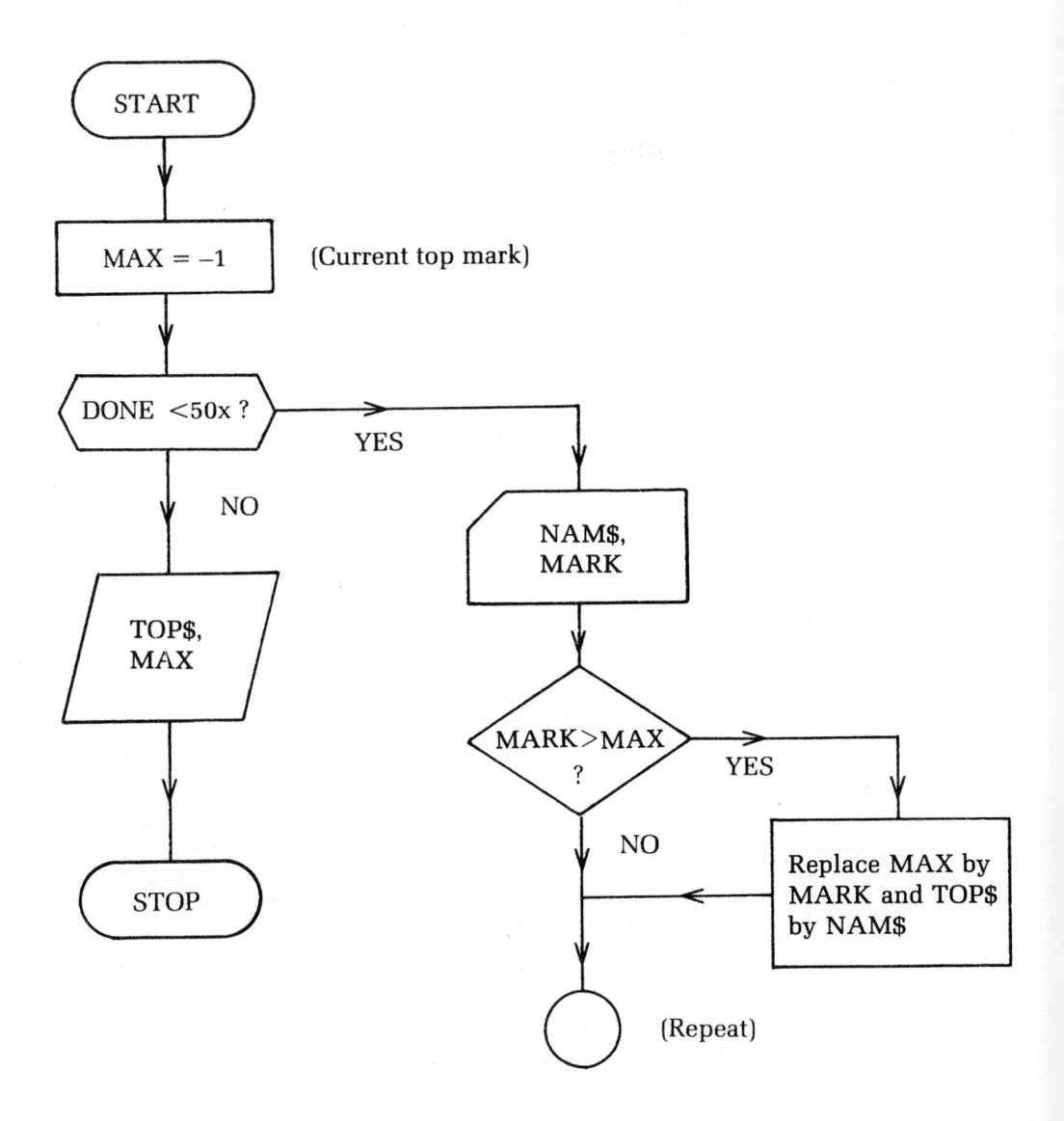

```
START
  │
  ▼
┌─────────────┐
│  MAX = -1   │   (Current top mark)
└─────────────┘
  │
  ▼
⬡ DONE <50x ? ⬡ ──YES──┐
  │                     │
  NO                    ▼
  │              ┌──────────┐
  ▼              │  NAM$,   │
┌─────────┐      │  MARK    │
│ TOP$,   │      └──────────┘
│ MAX     │           │
└─────────┘           ▼
  │              ◇ MARK>MAX ◇ ──YES──┐
  ▼                   ?              │
STOP                  │              ▼
                      NO     ┌──────────────────┐
                      │      │ Replace MAX by   │
                      │ ◄────│ MARK and TOP$    │
                      │      │ by NAM$          │
                      ▼      └──────────────────┘
                     ○  (Repeat)
```

Note that we have assumed that there is only one highest mark. The problem of what to do when two or more students share the top mark is discussed in Chapter Nine (Arrays).

3.5. Structure Plans

This is an alternative method of program preparation, which has advantages when the equivalent flowchart gets rather big. The plan may be written at a number of levels, of increasing complexity, as the logical structure of the program is developed.

For example, a first level plan for the highest mark problem in the previous section might be a simple statement of the problem:

1. Start
2. Initialise top mark
3. Find top student and top mark
4. Print top student and top mark.

Step 3 needs elaborating, so a more detailed plan might be:

1. Start
2. Initialise top mark
3. Repeat 50 times
   3.1. Input name and mark
   3.2. If mark > top mark then
      3.2.1. Replace top mark with mark
      3.2.2. Replace top student with name
4. Print top student and top mark.

There are no hard and fast rules about flowcharts or structure plans, and you should use whichever method you prefer. The essential point is to cultivate the mental discipline of getting the logic of a program clear BEFORE bothering about the detailed coding and rushing to the computer. The "top down" approach of flowcharts or structure plans means that the overall structure of a program is clearly thought out before you have to worry about the details of syntax, and this reduces the number of logical errors enormously.

Even the most ardent proponents of BASIC agree that it is an "unstructured" language:

> "It may not be as efficient as the FORTRAN language for a scientific problem, but it can solve the problem. BASIC is a loose and unstructured language, unlike Pascal which makes you think first and program later. But this freedom to roam around in the program makes the code friendlier."
> (Galanter, 1983, p. 75)

It is precisely this "freedom to roam around in the program" which makes it so easy to get into massive logical tangles, or "spaghetti", when writing complex BASIC programs. It is therefore doubly important to plan your program carefully beforehand, although many programmers steadfastly resist such an approach, in particular Galanter, who asserts:

> "In the opinion of a large and vocal minority of programming instructors, BASIC does not qualify as a really good programming language because it does not foster structured programming. To grasp the flavour of this criticism, you must understand that these instructors want more thinking

before you sit down at the machine. Their notion is that 'efficiency' is improved by preplanning the form of the program. Such preplanning can be done using BASIC just as well as it can using a structured language like Pascal. But the critics' point is that the language does not force you to plan in advance, which a language like Pascal does." (Op. cit. p. 154)

I am definitely one of those instructors who "want more thinking before you sit down at the machine"!

REFERENCE

Ellis, T.M.R. *A Structured Approach to FORTRAN 77 Programming*, Addison-Wesley, London, 1982.

Galanter, E. *Kids and Computers (The Parents' Microcomputer Handbook)*, Kingfisher Books, London, 1983, reprinted by permission of The Putnam Publishing Group.

3.6 EXERCISES

3.1 Work through the following structure plan, which defines a geometric construction:

1. Draw two perpendicular x- and y-axes
2. Draw the points A (10; 0) and B (0; 1)
3. While A does not coincide with the origin repeat
   3.1 Draw the straight line joining A and B
   3.2. Move A one unit to the left along the x-axis
   3.3. Move B one unit up on the y-axis
4. Stop.

3.2 Consider the following structure plan, where M and N are BASIC integer variables:

1. Set M = 44 and N = 28
2. While M <>N repeat
   2.1. While M > N repeat
      2.1.1. Replace M by M − N
   2.2. While N > M repeat
      2.2.1. Replace N by N − M
3. Print M

(a) Sketch the contents of M and N during execution, and give the output.
(b) Repeat (a) for M = 14 and N = 24.
(c) What general arithmetic procedure does the structure plan achieve (try more values of M and N if necessary)?

4 STRUCTURED PROGRAMS: GOSUB

BASIC has a construction called a subroutine which enables one to use a given set of statements repeatedly from different places in a program. Subroutines may also be used to write "structured" programs, i.e. programs where each logical section may easily be identified by someone reading the program. The general syntax is illustrated below.

4.1. The GOSUB Statement

```
100   GOSUB 500
110   ....
  .
  .
213   GOSUB 500
214   ....
  .
  .
480   END
490
500   REM SUBROUTINE STARTS HERE
  .
  .
550   RETURN                          'END OF SUBROUTINE
```

The set of statements constituting the subroutine are in lines 500 to 550 (in this example). On RUN, the GOSUB 500 encountered in line 100 causes the computer to go to line 500 for its next instruction, but to "remember" the line number of the GOSUB statement (line 100). The statements in lines 500 to 550 are then executed. On reaching RETURN in line 550, the machine "remembers" that it came from line 100, so it returns to the statement in the next line (number 110) and proceeds as usual from there. The next GOSUB 500 in line 213 causes lines 500 to 550 to be executed again, but this time on return it goes back to line 214. This may be repeated with as many GOSUB 500's as are required. The END statement in line 480 is necessary to prevent an unwanted execution of the subroutine.

Note:

1) A program may have many subroutines, all obviously starting on different line numbers, and all with their own RETURNs.

2) Subroutines may be defined recursively, i.e. they may call themselves. The next program segment uses the subroutine in lines 500 to 550 to print a variable number (N) of asterisks on a line. Such a subroutine could be very useful in a larger program to print a bar chart.

```
100   N = 20
110   GOSUB 500
```

```
120  N = 53
130  GOSUB 500
150  END
160
500  REM PRINT N ASTERISKS HERE
510  FOR I = 1 TO N
520      PRINT " * ";
530  NEXT I
540  PRINT                              'otherwise they will all be on one line!
550  RETURN
```

Note that all variables in a subroutine are "global" (i.e. there are no dummy variables in subroutines in BASIC) so any variable assigned in a subroutine has that value throughout the program.

4.2. Example: Company Payroll

The problem to print a company payroll, which was flowcharted in §3.3, may be programmed with two subroutines as follows:

```
010  REM * ***********************************************************************
020  REM * PRINTS COMPANY PAYROLL.                                                *
030  REM * SENIORS GET  1000 + 5% COMM, JUNIORS  750 + 3%                         *
040  REM * DATA CARDS HAVE NAME, SALES,                                           *
050  REM * AND RANK CODE (1 = SENIOR, 2 = JUNIOR)                                 *
060  REM * ***********************************************************************
070                         ,
080  REM CODE          : PAY CODE
090  REM I%            : COUNTER
100  REM NUM           : TOTAL NUMBER OF EMPLOYEES
110  REM PAY           : EMPLOYEE'S PAY
120  REM SALES         : EMPLOYEE'S SALES
130  REM TOT           : TOTAL SALARY BILL
140                         ,
150  REM NAM$          : EMPLOYEE'S NAME
160  REM RANK$         : EMPLOYEE'S RANK
170                         ,
180  TOT = 0
190  READ NUM
200  CLS
210  PRINT "NAME" TAB(15) "RANK" TAB(25) "SALES" TAB(35) "PAY"
220  PRINT
230                         ,
240  FOR I% = 1 TO NUM
250      READ NAM$, SALES, CODE
260      IF CODE = 1 THEN GOSUB 500
270      IF CODE = 2 THEN GOSUB 700
280      TOT = TOT + PAY
290      PRINT NAM$ TAB(15) RANK$ TAB(24) SALES TAB(34) PAY
300  NEXT I%
310                         ,
320  PRINT
330  PRINT "NUMBER OF EMPLOYEES:"; NUM
340  PRINT "TOTAL SALARY BILL :"; TOT
350  END
360                         ,
500  REM PROCESS SENIORS HERE
```

```
510   RANK$ = "SENIOR"
520   PAY = 1000 + 0.05 * SALES
530   RETURN
540                             '
700   REM PROCESS JUNIORS HERE
710   RANK$ = "JUNIOR"
720   PAY = 750 + 0.03 * SALES
730   RETURN
740                             '
800   DATA 3
810   DATA BAKER GN, 1028, 2
820   DATA JACKSON BR, 20000, 1
830   DATA SMITH GH, 2400, 1
```

The logical structure used in this example, where there are a number of different cases of a certain condition to be handled (i.e. of CODE), is sometimes called a CASE structure, and you should be able to recognise it when it occurs in a problem. The point is that the various cases of the condition should be mutually exclusive. The general structure is:

```
0010   IF cond1 THEN GOSUB 1000
0020   IF cond2 THEN GOSUB 2000
0030   IF cond3 THEN GOSUB 3000
         .
         .
0980   END
0990
1000   REM COME HERE UNDER CONDITION 1
         .
         .
1980   RETURN
         .
2000   REM COME HERE UNDER CONDITION 2
         .
2980   RETURN
         .
3000   REM COME HERE UNDER CONDITION 3
         .
         .
3980   RETURN
         .
         .
```

4.3. Example: Largest Number in a List

The problem of finding the top mark in a class, flowcharted in §3.4, may be programmed as follows, with one subroutine:

```
100   REM FINDS TOP MARK IN A LIST
105                             '
110   REM I%         : STUDENT COUNTER
120   REM MARK       : MARK
130   REM MAX        : TOP MARK
135                             '
```

```
140  REM NAM$       : NAME
150  REM TOP$       : TOP NAME
160  MAX = -1                   'top mark must be >= 0!
170                          ,
180  FOR I% = 1 TO 50
190     READ NAM$, MARK
200     IF MARK > MAX THEN GOSUB 500
210  NEXT I%
220                          ,
230  PRINT "TOP STUDENT:"; TOP$
240  PRINT "TOP MARK :"; MAX
250  END
260                          ,
500  REM KEEP THIS STUDENT'S NAME AND MARK
510  TOP$ = NAM$
520  MAX = MARK
530  RETURN
540                          ,
800  DATA JONES GR, 68
810  DATA SMITH IJ, 99
820  DATA THOMPSON RE, 12
```

Work through the program by hand for a few loops to check the logic.

4.4. EXERCISES

4.1 Write a program for the general solution of the quadratic equation
$ax^2 + bx + c = 0$.

Your program should be able to handle all possible values of the data a, b, and c (e.g. negative discriminant; $a = 0$; $a = b = 0$; etc.). (See Chapter Six for the square root function.)

4.2 Develop a structure plan for the solution of two simultaneous linear equations (i.e. two straight lines). Your algorithm must be able to handle all possible situations, viz. lines intersecting, parallel, or coincident. Write a program to implement your algorithm, and test it on some equations for which you know the answers. Hint: begin by deriving an algebraic formula for the solution of the system

$ax + by = c$
$dx + ey = f$.

5 LOOPS

The FOR-NEXT construction for repetition (§2.4) can only be used when the number of repetitions may be determined in advance, as in all the examples we have had so far. However, it often happens that the condition to end a loop is only satisfied during the execution of the loop itself. To program this sort of situation, we use a new statement: WHILE-WEND.

5.1. Conditional Loops

As an example consider a variation on the compound interest problem as programmed in §2.4. Suppose now that the interest is 5% p.a. The initial balance is $1000 again. We want to print out the year, the interest and the annual balance only while it is less than $.2000. The flowchart looks like this:

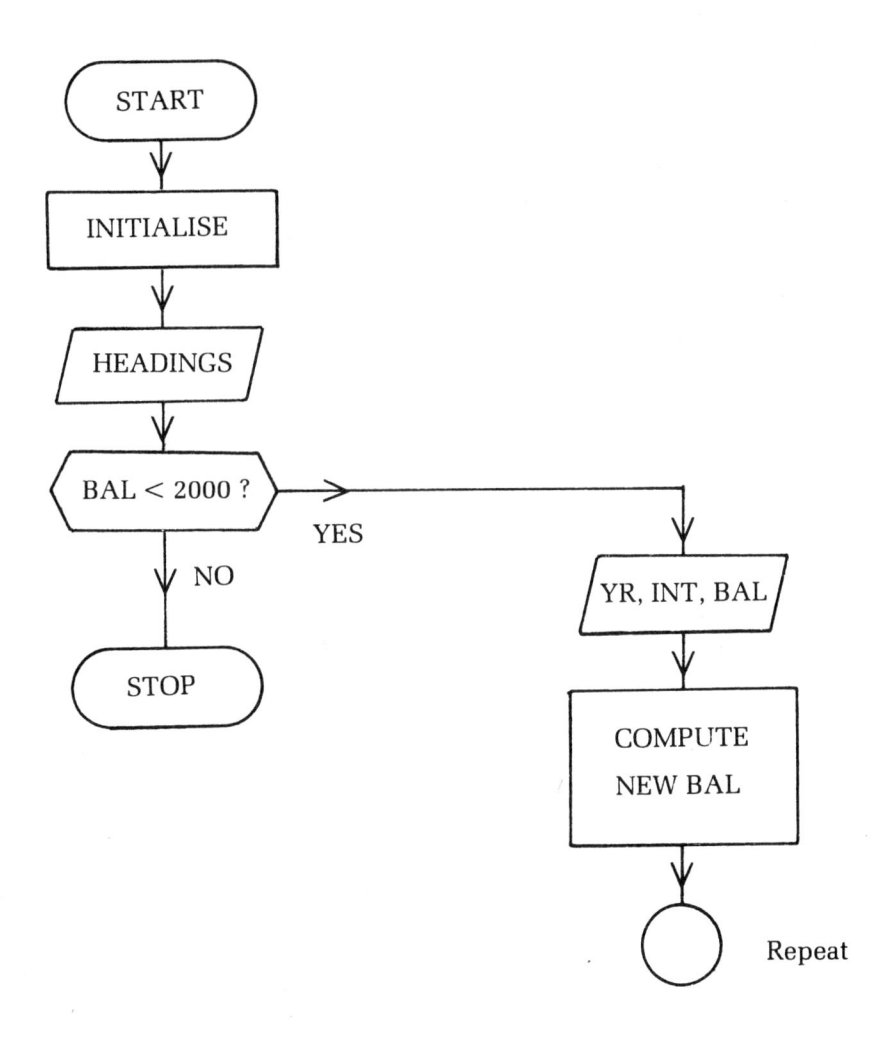

```
          START
            │
            ▼
        INITIALISE
            │
            ▼
        HEADINGS
            │
            ▼
       BAL < 2000 ? ──YES──►  YR, INT, BAL
            │                      │
            NO                     ▼
            │                 COMPUTE
            ▼                 NEW BAL
          STOP                    │
                                  ▼
                                 ○  Repeat
```

Alternatively, the structure plan for the same problem is:

    1. Start
    2. Initialise balance, year, rate, interest
    3. Print headings
    4. While balance < 2000 repeat
        4.1. Print year, interest, balance
        4.2. Compute new balance.

After all this preparation, the program almost writes itself:

```
100    BAL = 1000          'OPENING BALANCE
110    YEAR = 0
120    RATE = 0.05
130    INTR = 0            'INTEREST
140    CLS
150    PRINT "YEAR", "INTEREST, "BALANCE"
160                        '
170    WHILE BAL < 2000
180       PRINT YEAR, INTR, BAL
190       INTR = RATE * BAL
200       BAL = BAL + INTR
210       YEAR = YEAR + 1
220    WEND
230    END
RUN
```

YEAR	INTEREST	BALANCE
0	0	1000
1	50	1050
2	52.5	1102.5
3	55.125	1157.625
.		
.		
13	89.79281	1885.649
14	94.28246	1979.932

Note that you cannot use a FOR-NEXT loop here because you don't know how many repeats are going to be needed (14 in this case) until after the program has run!

It sometimes happens that you have to process an unknown amount of data. For example, suppose you want to compute the average mark for a class test, but you have no idea how many answer books you have, and you have no intention of counting them (in any case, you may make a mistake). You can get the computer to count them as follows. Assume that the lowest mark possible is zero. You can enter each student's name and mark, but when you reach the end enter a spurious name with a negative mark, such as

DUMMY, −1

Such a data item is called a sentinel or flag, since it flags the end of the data. The structure plan and program are as follows:

        1. Start
        2. Initialise
        3. Input name and mark

    4. While mark is >= 0 repeat
        4.1. Add mark to running total
        4.2. Add one to student counter
        4.3. Input name and mark
    5. Compute average mark
    6. Print total number in class and average mark.

```
100   TOT = 0                    'RUNNING TOTAL OF MARKS
110   NUM% = 0                   'STUDENT COUNTER
120   INPUT NAM$, MARK           'TO START THINGS UP
130                              '
140   WHILE MARK >= 0
150     TOT = TOT + MARK
160     NUM% = NUM% + 1
170     INPUT NAM$, MARK
180   WEND
190                              '
200   AVG = TOT / NUM%
210   PRINT "NUMBER OF STUDENTS:"; NUM%
220   PRINT "AVERAGE MARK: "; AVG
230   END
RUN
? ABLE ER, 45
? BAKER FT, 78
? SMITH BG, 56
? DUMMY, −1
NUMBER OF STUDENTS: 3
AVERAGE MARK:         59.66667
```

Note that we are assuming that there is at least one student in the class (can you amend the program to allow for an empty class?). We also have to INPUT the first data item before the conditional loop begins, to get things going. This is sometimes called a READ-AHEAD structure.

5.2. The WHILE and WEND Statements

The statements between WHILE and WEND are executed repeatedly, but only as long as the condition in the WHILE statement is true.

In general: n WHILE condition

                   .
                   .
               Statement(s) to be repeated
                   .
                   .
               m WEND

where "condition" is a logical expression, like

BAL < 2000

5.3. Summary: When to Repeat with WHILE-WEND

WHILE-WEND should be used to program a repeat structure when the exact number of repeats is NOT known in advance. Another way of saying this is that WHILE-WEND should be used to repeat whenever the CONDITION for repeating is

CHANGED in the body of the loop. This situation is characterized by the general structure plan as follows:

1. While CONDITION is TRUE repeat
    1.1. Statement(s) to be repeated.
    1.2. Reset CONDITION (if necessary)

5.4. Repeating with IF-GOTO

Some versions of BASIC do not have the WHILE-WEND compound statement. In that case, the problem of §5.1 may be programmed as follows (only lines 170 and 220 need to be changed):

```
170   IF BAL >= 2000 THEN GOTO 230
180      PRINT YEAR, INTR, BAL
190      INTR = RATE * BAL
200      BAL = BAL + INTR
210      YEAR = YEAR + 1
220   GOTO 170
230   END
```

Note that the condition expressed in line 170 is now the condition to STOP repeating (in which case the body of the loop is avoided with GOTO 230). This structure may be represented as follows:

1. Unless CONDITION to STOP is TRUE repeat
    1.1. Statement(s) to be repeated
    1.2. Reset CONDITION (if necessary).

The GOTO statement introduced here is the statement responsible for giving BASIC a bad name among programming purists because of the frightening ease with which an orderly structured program can be reduced to absolute chaos with statements like

GOTO anywhere

where "anywhere" is any line number in the program!

It is bad programming style to use GOTO under any circumstances other than the one described here (viz. a conditional loop), and then only if WHILE-WEND is not available. If you have WHILE-WEND in your version of BASIC, you should NEVER use GOTO!

5.5 Looping with FOR-NEXT

In this section, we look at more general uses of the FOR-NEXT construction.

5.5.1. Factorials

The counter in FOR-NEXT may be used in any expression inside the loop, as long as it (the counter) is not changed. The following program prints a table of n and $n!$ for values of n from 2 to 20 $(N! = 1 \times 2 \times ... \times (N - 1) \times N)$:

```
10   REM N!
20   FACT = 1
```

```
30  FOR N = 2 TO 20
40    FACT = FACT * N
50    PRINT N; FACT
60  NEXT N
70  END
```

5.5.2. The Binomial Coefficient

This is widely used in statistics. The number of ways of choosing r objects out of n without regard to order is given by:

$$\binom{n}{r} = \frac{n!}{r!(n-r)!} = \frac{n(n-1)(n-2)\ldots\ldots(n-r+1)}{r!}$$

e.g. $\binom{10}{3} = \frac{10!}{3! \times 7!} = \frac{10 \times 9 \times 8}{1 \times 2 \times 3}$

This may be computed as follows:

```
10  REM COMPUTES NCR
20  BIN = 1
30  INPUT N, R
40  FOR K% = 1 TO R
50    BIN = BIN * (N - K% + 1) / K%
60  NEXT K%
70  PRINT N; 'c'; R; '='; BIN
80  END
```

5.5.3. General

The counter in the FOR-NEXT loops in all the examples we have seen so far is increased by one every time by default. This may be changed, as we can see in the next program, which prints a table of *sin(x)* and *cos(x)* for x from 0° to 360°, in steps of 15°. (The special mathematical functions are dealt with in Chapter Six.)

```
10  PRINT "X", "SIN(X)", "COS(X)"
20  PRINT
30  CON = 3.141593 / 180    'TO CONVERT DEGREES TO RADIANS
40  FOR X = 0 TO 360 STEP 15
50    PRINT X, SIN( CON * X ), COS( CON *X )
60  NEXT X
70  END
```

In general: n   FOR N = J TO K STEP L

                     .

               m   NEXT N

Note:

1) If L > 0, the statements between lines n and m are executed repeatedly with N starting at J and increased by L each time until the statements have been executed for N having its greatest value NOT EXCEEDING K, e.g.

```
10   FOR N = 2 TO 7 STEP 2
20      PRINT N;
30   NEXT N
RUN
 2  4  6
```

2) If L > 0 and J > K, the statements are not executed at all, e.g.

```
10   FOR N = 5 TO 4
20      PRINT N;
30   NEXT
RUN
Ok      (i.e. no output since L = 1 by default)
```

3) If L < 0, the statements are executed until they have been executed with N having its smallest value which is not less than K, e.g.

```
10   FOR N = 5 TO 1 STEP −1
20      PRINT N;
30   NEXT N
RUN
 5  4  3  2  1
10   FOR N = 6 TO 1 STEP −2
20      PRINT N;
30   NEXT N
RUN
 6  4  2
```

4) If L < 0 and J < K, the statements are not executed at all.

5) J, K and L may be fractional, or may indeed stand for any valid BASIC expression, e.g.

```
10 FOR X = LOG( 1 ) TO LOG( 10 ) STEP LOG( 2 )
20    ....
```

6) If the counter in a FOR-NEXT loop changes by integer amounts, it will save computer time if the counter is an integer variable.

5.6. Example: Newton's Method to Find a Square Root

The square root X of any positive number A may be found using only the arithmetic operations of add, subtract, multiply and divide, with Newton's method, which is explained more fully in Chapter 14. The structure plan of the algorithm, and the program, are as follows:

1. Read A
2. Initialise X to 1
3. Repeat 6 times (say)
   3.1. X = (X + A / X) / 2.
   3.2. Print X
4. Stop.

```
10   REM SQUARE ROOTING WITH NEWTON
20   INPUT A              'NUMBER TO BE ROOTED
30   X = 1                'INITIAL GUESS
40
```

```
50   FOR I% = 1 TO 6
60     X = (X + A / X) / 2
70     PRINT X
80   NEXT I%
RUN
? 2
1.5
1.416667
1.414216
1.414214
1.414214
1.414214
```

The values of X "converge" to a limit, which is the square root of A. Most computers and calculators use a similar method internally to compute SQR and other intrinsic functions.

5.7. Example: Vertical Motion under Gravity

The example of §2.2, where a stone is projected vertically, may be amended with a FOR-NEXT statement to print the stone's displacement at regular intervals, say, of half a second:

```
100   REM VERTICAL DISPLACEMENT UNDER GRAVITY
110   CLS
120   PRINT "TIME", "DISPLACEMENT"
130   PRINT
140   G = 9.8
150   U = 60
160
170   FOR T = 0 TO 11 STEP 0.5
180     S = U * T - G / 2 * T ^ 2
190     PRINT T, S
200   NEXT T
210   END
```

5.8. Example: Regular Repayment of a Loan

The formula for the regular repayment of a loan over a fixed period at a given interest rate is given in Ex. 2.18. The following program uses a nested FOR-NEXT loop to print a table of the monthly repayments on a loan of $1000 over 15, 20 or 25 years, at interest rates that vary from 10% to 20% per annum. Since the formula is linear in the amount of the loan, the repayments on a loan of any amount may be found from the table below by simple proportion.

```
100   REM REGULAR LOAN REPAYMENT
110
120   A = 1000                       'PRINCIPAL
130   N = 12                         'NUMBER OF PAYMENTS PER YEAR
140   CLS
150   PRINT "RATE", " 15 YRS", " 20 YRS", " 25 YRS"
160   PRINT
170
180   FOR R = 0.1 TO 0.201 STEP 0.01
190     PRINT 100 * R; "%",
200     FOR K = 15 TO 25 STEP 5
```

```
210        P = R/N * A * (1 + R/N) ^ (N * K) / ( (1 + R/N) ^ (N * K) − 1 )
220        PRINT P,
230        NEXT K
240        PRINT
250    NEXT R
260    END
RUN
```

RATE	15 YRS	20 YRS	25 YRS
10 %	10.74607	9.650231	9.087017
11 %	11.36595	10.32187	9.801122
.			
.			
20 %	17.56297	16.98825	16.78452

5.9. Example: Computing the Limit of a Sequence

FOR-NEXT loops are ideal for computing successive members of a sequence. This example also highlights a problem that sometimes occurs when computing a limit. Consider the sequence

$$x(n) = a^n / n!, \; n = 1, 2, 3, \ldots$$

where a is any constant and $n! = n(n-1)(n-2)\ldots1$. The question is: what is the limit of this sequence as n gets indefinitely large. Let's take the case of $a = 10$. If we try to compute $x(n)$ directly we will soon be in trouble, because $n!$ gets large very rapidly as n increases, and a machine overflow occurs very quickly. However, the situation is neatly transformed if we spot that $x(n)$ may be formed from $x(n-1)$ as follows:

$$x(n) = a \, x(n-1) / n .$$

There are no overflow problems now. The following program computes $x(n)$ for $a = 10$, and increasing values of n, and prints it for $n = 10, 20, \ldots, 80$:

```
10   A = 10
20   X = 1
30   FOR N = 1 TO 80
40     X = A * X / N
50     IF N MOD 10 = 0 THEN PRINT N, X
60   NEXT N
```

The output is as follows:

```
10      2755.732
20      41.10318
30      3.769988E-03
40      1.225617E-08
50      3.287949E-15
60      1.201781E-22
70      8.348241E-31
80      0
```

From the results it appears that the limit of $x(n)$ as n gets indefinitely large is zero, and this may be proved mathematically. For more examples of calculus with computers, see Bitter (1983).

5.10. Summary: When to Repeat with FOR-NEXT

A FOR-NEXT loop should be used to program a repeat structure when the number of repeats is known to the program (i.e. in principle to the programmer) BEFORE the repeat structure is encountered. Another way of stating this is that a FOR-NEXT loop should be used to repeat whenever the CONDITION for repeating is UN-CHANGED in the body of the loop. This situation is characterized by the general structure plan:

    1. Repeat N times
        1.1. Statement(s) to be repeatead

where N is known or computed BEFORE step 1 is encountered, and is NOT changed by the statement(s) in step 1.1.

REFERENCE

Bitter G.G. *Microcomputer Applications for Calculus*, PWS Publishers, Boston, 1983.

5.11. EXERCISES

5.1   The compound interest program in §5.1 shows that an amount of $1000 will double in about 14 years with an interest rate of 5%. Using the same interest rate, run the program with initial balances of $500, $1500, $2000 and $10000 (say) to see how long they take to double. Your answer may surprise you.

5.2   Write a program to compute the sum of the integers 1 to 100. Hint: use a FOR-NEXT loop.

5.3   Write a program to compute the sum of the series
$1 + 1/2 + 1/3 + ... + 1/100$.

5.4   Write a program to compute the sum of the series
$1 + 2 + 3 + ...$
such that the sum is as large as possible without exceeding 100. The program should print out how many integers are used. Hint: use WHILE-WEND.

5.5   There are many formulae for computing π (the ratio of a circle's circumference to its diameter). The simplest is

$$\pi/4 = 1 - 1/3 + 1/5 - 1/7 + 1/9 - ... \tag{1}$$

which comes from the series

$$arctan(x) = x - x^3/3 + x^5 - x^7/7 + x^9/9 - ... \tag{*}$$

by letting $x = 1$.

    (a) Write a program to compute π using series (1). Use as many terms in the series as your computer system will reasonably allow (start modestly, with 100 terms, say, and rerun your program with more and more each time). You should find that the series "converges" very slowly, i.e. it takes a lot of terms to get fairly close to π.

    Re-arranging the series speeds up the convergence:

$$\pi/8 = 1/(1\times3) + 1/(5\times7) + 1/(9\times11) + ... \qquad (2)$$

(b) Write a program to compute π using series (2) instead. You should find that you need fewer terms to reach the same level of accuracy that you got in (a).

One of the fastest series used to compute π is

$$\pi/4 = 6\, arctan\,(1/8) + 2\, arctan\,(1/57) + arctan\,(1/239). \qquad (3)$$

(c) Use formula (3) to compute π. Don't use the function ATN to compute the arctangents, since that would be cheating. Rather use the series (*) above.

5.6 The transcendental number e (= 2.71828182....) can be shown to be the limit of

$$1 / (1 - x)^{1/x}$$

as x tends to zero (from above). Write a program which shows how this expression converges to e as x gets closer and closer to zero.

5.7 A man borrows $10000 to buy a used car. Interest on his loan is compounded at the rate of 2% per month while the outstanding balance is greater than $5000, and at 1% per month otherwise. He pays back $300 every month, except for the last month when the repayment must be less than $300. He pays at the end of each month, after the interest on the balance has been compounded. The first repayment is made one month after the loan is paid out to him. Write a program which prints out a monthly statement of the balance (after the monthly payment has been made), what the final payment will be, and how long it will take to pay back the loan. Hint: use WHILE-WEND. Answer: $157.75 in the 54th month (don't forget the interest in the final month).

5.8 The exponential function may be expressed mathematically as a Taylor series:

$$exp(x) = 1 + x + x^2/2! + x^3/3! + ...$$

Write a program which uses this series to compute exp(x). Arrange for the series to stop once the general term is less than 1E-6 (i.e. only use terms that are not less than 1E-6). Compare your answer with the BASIC function EXP(X) described in Chapter Six. Hint: use WHILE-WEND.

5.9 The formula in §2.3.1 gives the value of an investment A after interest has been compounded n times a year for k years. Write a program to compute the value of the investment as n gets larger and larger, i.e. as the compounding periods become more and more frequent, like daily, hourly, and ultimately instantaneously (?). Use the same values as in §2.3.1, viz. $A = 1000, r = 4\%$ and $k = 10$ years. You should observe that your output gradually approaches a limit (which is revealed in Ex. 6.3).

6 SPECIAL FUNCTIONS

Most calculators have special function keys (sine, cosine, log, etc.) and BASIC has the equivalent of these also. For example, if X is a variable, to find the sine of the value in X, we simply use the statement

n   Y = SIN(X)

where Y is another variable. A comprehensive list of special functions available in Microsoft BASIC appears in Appendix E. The more commonly used ones are given below.

6.1. List of Special Functions

In the following list, any BASIC variable or expression may be used as an argument of a function (where the function requires an argument). The function may appear in a program wherever a BASIC variable or expression may legitimately be used. X and X$ stand for numeric and string expressions respectively. Arguments for the trigonometric functions must be expressed in radians (to convert degrees to radians multiply by $\pi/180$ where $\pi = 3.141593$).

ABS(X)   absolute value of X.

ASC(X$)   ASCII code for first character in X$ (see Appendix F for the ASCII codes), e.g.
PRINT ASC("A")
65

ATN(X)   arctan(X) in radians.

CHR$(X)   character with ASCII code X, e.g.
PRINT CHR$(64)
@

CINT(X)   rounds to nearest integer, e.g.
PRINT CINT (45.67); CINT(−2.89)
46 −3

COS(X)   cosine of X.

CSRLIN   cursor line position.

DATE$ system date, in American notation (on the IBM PC).

EXP(X)   e to the power of X.

FIX(X)   truncates by chopping off decimal part, e.g.
PRINT FIX (45.67); FIX (−2.89)
45 −2

INT(X)   largest integer not exceeding X, e.g.
PRINT INT (45.67); INT (−2.89)
45 −3

LEN(X$) length of the string X$.

LOG(X)   natural logarithm of X.

POS(X)   cursor column position (X is a dummy argument).

RND   uniformly distributed random number, between 0 and 1 (exclusive).

SIN(X)   sine of X.

SPC(X)   prints X spaces on the screen or printer when used in PRINT or LPRINT respectively.

SQR(X)   the square root of X, where $X \geq 0$.

TAB(N)   sets the next print position to column N.

TAN(X)   tangent of X.

TIME$ system time as an eight character string, "hh:mm:ss".

TIMER   system time in seconds elapsed since midnight or System Reset.

VAL(X$) numeric value of the string X$, e.g.
         PRINT VAL("1984") − 1
            1983

6.2. Example: Projectile Motion

Write a program to compute the position (x- and y-coordinates) and velocity (magnitude and direction) of a projectile, given t, the time since launch; u, the launch velocity; a, the initial angle of launch (in degrees); and g, the acceleration due to gravity.

The horizontal displacement is given by the formula

$x = u.cos(a)t$

and the vertical displacement by

$y = u.sin(a)t - gt^2/2$.

The velocity has magnitude V such that

$V^2 = [u.cos(a)]^2 + [u.sin(a) - gt]^2$,

and makes an angle θ with the ground such that

$tan(\theta) = [u.sin(a) - gt]/[u.cos(a)]$.

The program is:

```
100   READ ANG, G, T, U
110   ANG = ANG * 3.14159 / 180                    'CONVERT TO RADIANS
120   X = U * COS( ANG ) * T
130   Y = U * SIN( ANG ) * T - G * T ^ 2 / 2
140   VX = U * COS( ANG )
150   VY = U * SIN( ANG ) - G * T
160   V = SQR( VX * VX + VY * VY )
170   THETA = ATN( VY / VX )
```

```
180  PRINT "Y: "; Y, "X: "; X
190  PRINT "V: "; V, "THETA: "; THETA
200  DATA 60, 9.8, 10, 60
RUN
Y: 29.61499    X: 300.0004
V: 54.9504     THETA: −.9932765
```

Note that the projectile is on the way down.

6.3 EXERCISES

6.1 Write some BASIC statements which will:

(a) find the length C of the hypotenuse of a right-angled triangle in terms of the lengths A and B of the other two sides;

(b) find the length C of a side of a triangle given the lengths A and B of the other two sides and the size in degrees of the included angle THETA, using the cosine rule.

6.2 If a random variable X is distributed normally with zero mean and unit standard deviation, the probability that $0 \leq X \leq x$ is given by the standard normal function $\Phi(x)$. This is usually looked up in tables, but it may be approximated as follows:

$$\Phi(x) = 0.5 - r(at + bt^2 + ct^3),$$

where $a = 0.4361836$
$b = -0.1201676$
$c = 0.937298$
$r = \exp(-0.5 x^2)/\sqrt{2\pi}$
$t = 1/(1 + 0.3326x)$

Write a program to compute and print out values of $\Phi(x)$ for $0 \leq x \leq 4$ in steps of 0.1.

6.3 Write a program to compute the value of the formula

$A \exp(rk)$

for $A = 1000, r = 0.04$ and $k = 10$ and compare your answer with the output of Ex. 5.9. What do you conclude?

6.4 If a loan A is repaid in equal instalments of P paid n times a year, where the nominal annual interest rate is r, the period k (in years) to repay the entire loan is given by

$k = 1/n \log(P/(P - rA/n))/\log(1 + r/n).$

Write a program to compute the repayment period of a loan of $50 000, where the payments are made monthly, and the interest rate is 20% per annum. Run the program for some different values of P, and observe that the program will not work if $P < \$833$. Can you explain this?

7   ERRORS

Programs seldom run correctly the first time, even for experienced programmers! In computer jargon, an error in a program is called a "bug", and the process of detecting and eradicating them is called "debugging". There are four main types of error: syntax, execution, rounding and logic.

7.1. Syntax Errors

These are errors in the code, like spelling mistakes. The BASIC interpreter (i.e. the master program which translates your BASIC code into machine code which the computer can understand) will tell you where the synataх errors are, e.g.

```
10   X = 9,8
RUN
Syntax error in 10
Ok
10   X = 9,8
```

Unfortunately it doesn't tell you where exactly in the line the error is (9,8 should be 9.8). All it manages is to display the errant line again with the cursor on the extreme left ready for you to correct.

Sometimes the errors are rather subtle, e.g.

```
10   FNL = 1
RUN
Syntax error in 10
```

The problem here is that the letters FN are reserved and should signal a user function (see Chapter 11). But sometimes the interpreter is more helpful:

```
10   Y = X + FNL
RUN
Undefined user function in 10
```

The next one is also rather mysterious:

```
10   INPUT NAME$, MARK
RUN
? SMITH GB, 98
Syntax error in 10
```

It's hard to see the error! In such cases it helps to use "direct mode" to print the variables concerned, e.g.

```
PRINT NAME$
Syntax error
```

This shows that the problem is with NAME$. The reason is that NAME is a reserved word, and although you are allowed to embed reserved words, you may not tag a type declaration character ($, %, ! or #) on the end of a reserved word.

But there are cases when the interpreter is more explicit, e.g.

```
10   FOR I = 1 TO 10
20      PRINT I;
30   END
RUN
FOR without NEXT in 10
```

7.2. Execution Errors

These are errors which occur while the program is running. Execution is interrupted, and the program returns to command level with the "Ok" prompt, e.g.

```
10   X = -1
20   Y = SQR( X )
RUN
Illegal function call in 20
```

At least that one's quite clear. So is this one:

```
10   X = 0
20   Y = 1 / X
RUN
Division by zero
```

A useful tip is that when a crash occurs, the variables all retain their values up to that point. So you can PRINT any variables you wish to, in order to track down the error, e.g.

```
10   COT = COS( A ) / SIN( A )
RUN
Division by zero
PRINT A
   0
```

Since A is undefined it is taken to be zero, and sine(0) is zero. Microsoft BASIC has a facility called a "trace" which can be useful in debugging. The command TRON prints the line numbers in order of execution when the program is run. TROFF switches the trace off again. E.g.:

```
10   N = 5
20   FOR I = N * 2 to N / 2 STEP -2
30      PRINT I
40   NEXT I
50   END
TRON
Ok
RUN
[10] [20] [30] 10
[40] [30]  8
[40] [30]  6
[40] [30]  4
[40] [50]
Ok
TROFF
```

The numbers in square brackets are the line numbers in order of execution; the numbers not in brackets are the values printed by the program.

7.3. Rounding Error

At times the computer gives numerical answers to a problem which appear inexplicably different from what we know to be the correct mathematical answers. This can be due to rounding error, which results from the finite precision available on the computer, e.g. 32 bits per variable instead of an infinite number. For example, in the next program simple arithmetic shows that B and C should be equal (to 16), and consequently that their difference should be zero. But this is not the case, because the recurring decimals resulting from dividing by 7 are rounded in the computer's memory:

```
10   C = 16
20   B = C / 7 * 7
30   PRINT B - C
40   IF B = C THEN PRINT "NUMBERS EQUAL"
RUN
-9.536743E-07
Ok
```

This example also illustrates the difficulty of testing non-integer variables for equality: the test often fails because of rounding error. A safer test is

```
40   IF ABS( B - C ) < = 1E-6 THEN PRINT "NUMBERS ALMOST EQUAL"
```

Rounding error can be significantly reduced (or even eliminated) by using double precision variables. Such variables use eight bytes of memory, are stored with 17 digits of precision, and are printed with up to 16 digits. A variable is specified with type double precision by tagging the number sign (#) on at the end of its name. The declaration DEFDBL may also be used, e.g. the statement

```
5   DEFDBL A-Z
```

in the previous program will specify all variables in it with double precision type. If this is done, the difference B-C is computed as exactly zero.

Rounding error may also be reduced by a mathematical rearrangement of the problem. If the well known quadratic equation is written in the less usual form

$x^2 - 2ax + e = 0$

the two solutions may be expressed as

```
X1 = A + SQR( A * A - E ) and
X2 = A - SQR( A * A - E )
```

If E is very small compared to A the second root is expressed as the difference between two nearly equal numbers, and considerable significance is lost. E.g. taking A = 5000 and E = 1 gives X2 as zero exactly in BASIC. However, the second root may also be expressed mathematically as

```
X2 = E / ( A + SQR ( A * A - E ))
```

which is approximately equal to E / (2 * A). Using this form in BASIC gives X2 as 0.0001, which is most certainly not the same as zero.

Rounding error is discussed further in Chapter 14 in the section on numerical differentiation.

7.4. Errors of Logic

These are the most subtle errors. The program runs happily, but the answers are wrong! The worst cases are when you don't realise that the answers are wrong. Always try to run the program for some special cases where you know the answers. Otherwise try to use your insight into the problem to check whether the answers seem to be of the right order of magnitude.

The only way to correct logical errors is to go back to the planning stage and examine your algorithm with a flowchart or structure plan. Also try working through the program by hand to see if you can spot where things start going wrong.

8 ADVANCED INPUT/OUTPUT

Up to now we have used simple PRINT or LPRINT statements to print program results. The overall effect has not always been pleasing to the eye, since we generally prefer to right justify integers (i.e. blank fill from the left) over fewer than 14 columns, and we usually want to restrict the number of decimal places printed. This may be done with the PRINT USING statement.

8.1. PRINT USING: Numeric Fields

The basic idea is that you can specify in a PRINT statement a "mask" or "image" of how the output must look, e.g.

```
10   X = 123.4567
20   PRINT USING "###.#"; X;
30   PRINT USING "#####"; X
RUN
123.5   123
```

The general syntax is

PRINT USING v$; list of expressions [;]

where v$ is a string constant or variable consisting of special formatting characters which determine how the expressions will be printed. Note that a comma should not be used at the end of the PRINT USING statement. The rules for commas and semi-colons in the PRINT statement do not apply to PRINT USING, which is a totally different statement.

8.1.1. The # Formatting Character

Each # (number symbol) represents a digit position in the output field. A decimal point may be inserted in the formatting field. If the number to be printed does not fill the field it is right justified. E.g.

```
10   X = 12.3446
20   Y = 123
30   PRINT USING "###.##"; X, Y
RUN
 12.34123.00
Ok
30   PRINT USING "#####"; X, Y
RUN
    12   123
```

The next example shows how string constants may be included in the formatting field, and also how to use TAB in this context. Note that TAB must be in a PRINT statement on a separate line.

```
10   X = 6.45
20   Y = 7.34
```

```
30  PRINT USING "X=##.#"; X;
40  PRINT TAB( 10 )
50  PRINT USING "Y=##.#"; Y
RUN
X= 6.5   Y= 7.3
```

Another possibility is:

```
10  A = 1.2
20  B = 3.4
30  PRINT USING "THE SUM OF ##.# AND ##.# IS ##.#"; A; B; A + B
RUN
THE SUM OF  1.2  AND  3.4  IS  4.6
```

If the number to be printed is too large for the field, it is preceded by a % symbol, e.g.

```
10  X = 123.456
20  PRINT USING "##.##"; X
RUN
%123.46
```

8.1.2. The + Formatting Character

A plus sign at the beginning (or end) of the format string causes the sign of the number to be printed before (or after) the number, e.g.

```
10  X = -12.345
20  Y = 99.76
30  PRINT USING "+###.#"; X, Y
RUN
 -12.3 +99.8
```

8.1.3. The $$ Formatting Characters

A double dollar sign on the left of the format field causes a dollar sign to be printed on the left of the number. Two extra positions are specified, one of which is for the dollar sign, e.g.

```
10  X = 99.99
20  PRINT USING "NOW ONLY$$###.##?"; X
RUN
NOW ONLY  $99.99?
```

8.1.4. Exponential Format

Four caret (^) symbols placed at the end of the formatting string cause the number to be printed in floating point scientific notation. The number of characters printed before and after the decimal point is controlled by the format string, e.g.

```
10  X = 123456.78
20  PRINT USING "###.###^^^^"; X
RUN
  12.346E+04
10  X=-1.23456E-4
RUN
 -12.346E-05
```

8.1.5. The _ Formatting Character

An underscore character in the format string prints the next character literally. This is useful for printing the formatting characters themselves, e.g.

```
10   X = 99.99
20   PRINT USING "NOW ONLY$$###.##_!"; X
RUN
NOW ONLY  $99.99!
```

8.2. PRINT USING: String Fields

There are two main formatting characters that may be used to print strings with PRINT USING.

8.2.1. The ! Formatting Character

This symbol specifies that only the first character in the given string be printed, e.g.

```
10   N$ = "OH"
20   PRINT USING "!"; N$
RUN
O
```

8.2.2. The \\ Formatting Characters

This seems rather curious at first. If there are n spaces between the back slashes, n+2 characters from the string are printed. If the string is too long, the leftmost significant characters are printed. If the string is too short, it is blank filled from the right. E.g.

```
10   A$ = "JAMES"
20   B$ = "JOHN"
30   PRINT USING " \      \"; A$;
40   PRINT USING "\\"; B$
RUN
JAMES JO
```

Note also that string constants may be printed in the same line.

8.3 The LPRINT USING Statement

This works exactly like PRINT USING except that output is sent to the printer.

8.4. Files: Updating Student Records

Output from a BASIC program may be sent to a file which resides permanently on a diskette, and input may also be fetched from such a file. This facility provides a means of keeping records which constantly need to be updated or examined and analysed. In this section we are going to look at an example which will carry through to the next chapter: initializing and updating a student record file which contains a list of students with their marks for various course offerings. We begin with writing a list of names to a file.

8.4.1. Sending Output to a File: WRITE

An output file (output from the point of view of the program running in the computer's memory) must first be opened as an output file, and the file name must be connected to a file number, which is used in the WRITE # statement, e.g.

n   OPEN "RECORD" FOR OUTPUT AS #1

The subsequent statement

m   WRITE #1, X

will output the variable X to the file RECORD instead of to the screen or printer. The previous contents of RECORD is lost. When all the date has been sent, the file must be closed with the statement

n   CLOSE #1

In Microsoft BASIC the default maximum number of files that can be open at any one time is three.

In all the file handling examples throughout the rest of this book it is assumed that you are using a computer with a single disk drive. If you have more than one disk drive, and prefer to use drive B, say, for program input and output, simply replace all references in what follows to "FILENAME" by B:FILENAME", or use string concatenation:

```
10  FIL$ = "PLONK"
20  BFIL$ = "B:" + FIL$
30  OPEN BFIL$ FOR OUTPUT AS #2
    ....
```

The following program writes a list of names, of any length, to the file RECORD, which may or may not already exist. If it does already exist, its current contents will be destroyed. The program continues accepting names until the flag "DUMMY" is input:

```
10  REM WRITES NAMES TO FILE
20  OPEN "RECORD" FOR OUTPUT AS #1
30  INPUT N$
35
40  WHILE N$ <> "DUMMY"
50     WRITE #1, N$
60     INPUT N$
70  WEND
75
80  CLOSE #1
90  END
RUN
? ABLE ER
? BAKER IJ
? SMITH ZZ
? DUMMY
Ok
```

The file RECORD should now have three names in it, but it would be nice to check! The next little program, which is called READ.BAS for future reference, reads any file, line by line, and prints the entire contents of each line, irrespective of delimiting commas, etc:

```
10   REM READS FILE AS IT IS
20   OPEN "RECORD" FOR INPUT AS #1
25
30   WHILE NOT EOF( 1 )
40     LINE INPUT #1, L$
50     PRINT L$
60   WEND
65
70   CLOSE #1
80   END
SAVE "READ"
RUN
"ABLE ER"
"BAKER IJ"
"SMITH ZZ"
```

Note that the WRITE # statement in the first program has enclosed the strings in quotes. We will return to this later. The program above introduces a number of new features.

1. The file RECORD now has to be OPENed for INPUT, instead of OUTPUT (line 20) because the program must look in this file for its input.

2. The EOF function in line 30 returns a "true" value (-1) as soon as the end of the file (#1 here) has been encountered. In general EOF(n) is true (-1) if the end of file #n has been reached, and false (0) if not.

3. As long as EOF(1) in line 30 is not true the program executes the statement in line 40, which inputs the entire line as a string of characters (including delimiting commas). The LINE INPUT # statement is very useful for this purpose. In general the statement

    n   LINE INPUT #m S$

    inputs the next line from file #m into the string S$.

We are now ready to update our student file RECORD by inputting some test results. To do this we will open a new (dummy) file called SCRATCH. We will then read the names from RECORD, input each student's mark from the computer terminal, and write each student's name and mark to the dummy file SCRATCH. When all the marks have been entered SCRATCH will actually contain the updated student record, which we wanted to be in RECORD. However, we can get round this neatly by renaming the file SCRATCH as RECORD, but before we do this we must destroy the old version of RECORD. The next program does all this:

```
100   REM UPDATES LIST BY ADDING MARKS
110   OPEN "RECORD" FOR INPUT AS #1
120   OPEN "SCRATCH" FOR OUTPUT AS #2
125
130   WHILE NOT EOF( 1 )
140     INPUT #1, N$
150     PRINT N$; "   ";
160     INPUT MK
```

```
170    WRITE #2, N$, MK
180    WEND
185
190    CLOSE #1
200    KILL "RECORD"
210    CLOSE #2
220    NAME "SCRATCH" AS "RECORD"
230    END
RUN
ABLE ER ? 78
BAKER IJ ? 0
SMITH ZZ ? 99
Ok
```

Note:

1. The INPUT #1 statement in line 140 behaves exactly like INPUT except that the program looks in file #1 for the input instead of at the screen. In contrast to LINE INPUT #1, INPUT #1 interprets commas as delimiters between values to be input.

2. The NAME statement in line 220 renames the files appropriately. Note that RECORD must first be killed. If there is a power failure after line 200 has been executed, but before line 220 has been executed, your updated record file should still be intact under the name SCRATCH! In general,

   n   NAME "OLDFILE" AS "NEWFILE"

renames OLDFILE as NEWFILE. OLDFILE must exist on the diskette, and NEWFILE must not exist on the diskette (which is why it is necessary to KILL the previous version first).

To check that all this impressive file manipulation has really worked we can run the program READ.BAS, which uses LINE INPUT # to read each line in the file RECORD:

```
RUN "READ"
"ABLE ER", 78
"BAKER IJ", 0
"SMITH ZZ", 99
Ok
```

Note that the WRITE # statement inserts quotes and commas into the file. This is so that the file can subsequently be read with INPUT. If PRINT # is used instead of WRITE # the program prints into the file exactly as PRINT would print on the screen: without quotes and commas. But then we wouldn't be able to read the file with INPUT. Similarly, the WRITE statement prints on the screen with enclosing quotes and delimiting commas.

Our program READ.BAS certainly gives us the information in the student record file, but the layout leaves much to be desired. The following program reads the same file, but produces a more pleasing format:

```
100    REM READS FILE AND PRINTS NEAT FORMATTED OUTPUT
110    OPEN "RECORD" FOR INPUT AS #1
120    N = 10
```

```
130  FMT$ = " \ " + SPACE$(N) + " \ "
140  CLS
150  PRINT "NAME" TAB(N+3) "MARK"
160  PRINT
165
170  WHILE NOT EOF( 1 )
180     INPUT #1, N$, MK
190     PRINT USING FMT$; N$;
200     PRINT USING "###"; MK
210  WEND
215
220  CLOSE
230  END
RUN
NAME      MARK
ABLE ER    78
BAKER IJ    0
SMITH ZZ   99
```

The SPACE$(N) function in line 130 returns a string variable of N blanks. This in turn is used to construct a string format field of width N+2. In conjunction with TAB(N+3) when printing the headings, this ensures that the marks are all right justified and fall under the right heading.

8.5. EXERCISE

8.1 Rewrite the example of §5.8 to print the amounts correct to two decimal places.

9 ARRAYS

In this chapter we consider a very useful programming concept: subscripted variables.

9.1. Mean and Standard Deviation

We wish to compute the sample mean and standard deviation of a set of N observations. The mean is defined as

$$\overline{X} = \sum_{i=1}^{N} X_i / N$$

where X_i is the ith observation. There are two ways of expressing the standard deviation s. One is as follows:

$$s^2 = [\sum_{i=1}^{N} X_i^2 - N\overline{X}^2] / (N-1)$$

This form is used in the next program. The first DATA statement indicates how many observations there are: 10 in this case.

```
10   REM HERE WE GO AT STATS!
15   M = 0
17   S = 0
20   READ N                          'NUMBER OF OBSERVATIONS
30   FOR I = 1 TO N
40     READ X
50     M = M + X
60     S = S + X * X
70   NEXT I
80   REM NOW COMPUTE MEAN AND STD DEVIATION
90   M = M / N
100  S = SQR( (S - N * M * M) / (N - 1) )
110  PRINT "MEAN:" M TAB(20) "STD DEVIATION:"; S
120  DATA 10
130  DATA 5, 7, 6.8, 2, 8, 4.5, 7.4
140  DATA 8.9, 10, 4.2
999  END
```

Lines 50 and 60 compute running totals for M and S, so M, for example, will take the successive values 5, 12, 18.8, 20.8, etc.

A more familiar way, however, of expressing the standard deviation is by the formula

$$s^2 = \sum_{i=1}^{N} (X_i - \overline{X})^2 / (N - 1)$$

Programming this form introduces the concept of an ARRAY, or LIST. Suppose we now have 100 observations. They may be read into memory cells named X(1), X(2), ..., X(100), where X stands for any valid BASIC variable. The mean may be computed while the observations are being read in, as before. When all the data have been read, they remain in variables X(1), ... , X(100) for further use later on in the program. The standard deviation may now be found by computing the deviation of each X(I) from the mean as follows, using the second formula quoted above:

```
10   DIM X(100)            'DIMENSION DECLARATION
12   M = 0
13   S = 0
15   READ N
20   FOR I = 1 TO N
30     READ X(I)
40     M = M + X(I)
50   NEXT I
60   M = M / N              'COMPUTE MEAN
70   FOR I = 1 TO N
80     S = S + (X(I) - M) ^ 2
90   NEXT I
100  S = SQR( S / (N - 1) )
110  PRINT M; S
115  DATA 100
120  DATA 7, 8, 5.4, ....
130  DATA ......
140  DATA ......, 11.6
999  END
```

MEMORY

```
X (0):
X (1):   7
X (2):   8
X (3):   5.4
         :
X (100): 11.6
```

Note:

1) X above is called an ARRAY or LIST or SUBSCRIPTED VARIABLE.

2) The I in X(I) is called the SUBSCRIPT, and may be any valid BASIC expression, e.g.

   200 I = 25
   210 Z = X(I / 7)

   sets Z = X(4) because the subscript is rounded, not truncated.

3) The lowest subscript value is always zero by default. It can be set to one by the statement

   OPTION BASE 1

   at the start of the program, before any DIM statements. The highest value is the one declared in the DIM statement. So a reference, e.g., to X(102) in the above program will cause an error.

4) If an array is inadvertently not declared in a DIM statement, it is assumed to be dimensioned 10.

5) Particular members of the array are called ELEMENTS of the array.

ARRAYS

The next example shows how the subscript of an array may be used to store the first 10 even numbers in the array:

```
10   DIM X(10)
20   FOR I = 1 TO 10
30     X(I) = 2 * I
40   NEXT I
50   ....
```

9.2. Bar Charts and Frequency Distributions

Suppose we want a program to analyse the results of a test written by 40 students. We would like to know how many students obtained marks in the range 0% - 9%; 10% - 19%; ....; 90% - 99%; 100%+ (each of these ranges is called a decile). We will therefore need an array F, say, with 11 elements (locations), where each element stores the number of students with marks in that particular range, as follows:

Number scoring 0% – 9% stored in F(0) – 0th decile;
number scoring 10% – 19% stored in F(1) – 1st decile;
number scoring 20% – 29% stored in F(2) – 2nd decile;
....
number scoring 90% – 99% stored in F(9) – 9th decile;
number scoring 100%+ stored in F(10) – 10th decile.

So altogether there are ELEVEN deciles. The program needs to read each mark, and decide to which of the 11 deciles, or classes, that mark belongs:

```
10   DIM F(10)
20   FOR I = 1 TO 40
30     READ M
40     K = INT( M / 10 )            ' DECILE
50     F(K) = F(K) + 1              'ANOTHER MARK IN THE KTH DECADE
60   NEXT I
70   FOR I = 0 TO 10
75     PRINT F(I);
77   NEXT I
80   REM DATA FOLLOWING HERE
90   DATA 56,67,38,100,88,63,4,66,80,46,51,89,0,20,32,72
100  DATA 96,44,62,50,2,39,82,65,40,49,54,77,90,58,61,32,49
110  DATA 45,59,47,42,69,76,54
999  END
```

The output would be: 3 0 1 4 8 7 7 3 4 2 1

We can improve the program by making it print a bar chart of the frequencies F(I):

```
10   DIM F(10)
20   FOR I = 1 TO 40
30     READ M
40     K = INT( M / 10 )            'DECILE
50     F(K) = F(K) + 1              'ANOTHER MARK IN THE KTH DECADE
60   NEXT I
80   REM DATA FOLLOWING HERE
90   DATA 56,67,38,100,88,63,4,66,80,46,51,89,0,20,32,72
100  DATA 96,44,62,50,2,39,82,65,40,49,54,77,90,58,61,32,49
110  DATA 45,59,47,42,69,76,54
```

```
120   PRINT " BAR CHART OF TEST RESULTS"
130   PRINT
140   PRINT " RANGE" TAB(12) "NO. OF STUDENTS"
150   PRINT
160   FOR I = 0 TO 10
170     PRINT I * 10; "–"; 10 * I+9 TAB(12) F(I);
180     PRINT TAB(17);
190     FOR K = 1 TO F(I)
195       PRINT "*";
197     NEXT K
200     PRINT
210   NEXT I
999   END
```

The program now has the following output:

BAR CHART OF TEST RESULTS

RANGE	NO. OF STUDENTS	
0 – 9	3	***
10 – 19	0	
20 – 29	1	*
30 – 39	4	****
40 – 49	8	********
50 – 59	7	*******
60 – 69	7	*******
70 – 79	3	***
80 – 89	4	****
90 – 99	2	**
100 –109	1	*

NOTE that F(1) is zero, so that line 190 is effectively

```
190   FOR K = 1 TO 0
```

meaning that PRINT "*"; on the next line is not executed at all when there are no marks in a particular decile.

9.3. Sorting a List: the Bubble Sort

A standard application of arrays is in the problem of sorting a list of numbers into, let us say, ascending order. The basic idea is that the unsorted list is read into an array. The numbers are then ordered by a process which essentially passes through the list many times, swopping consecutive elements that are in the wrong order, until all the elements are in the right order. Such a process is called a Bubble Sort, since the smallest numbers rise to the top of the list, like bubbles of air in water. In fact, the largest number will "sink" to the bottom of the list after the first pass in the version shown below. There are many other methods of sorting (e.g. the Quick Sort), of varying degrees of efficiency (see, e.g. Cooke, Craven and Clarke, 1982).

A structure plan for a bubble sort is as follows:

1. Initialise N (length of list)
2. Read in the list (X)
3. Repeat N–1 times (on counter K):

3.1. Repeat N–K times on counter J:
   3.1.1. If X(J) > X(J+1) then
      3.1.1.1. Swop X(J) and X(J+1)
4. Print the list, which is now sorted.

As an example, consider a list of five numbers: 27, 13, 9, 5 and 3. They are initially read into the array X. The computer's memory for this problem is sketched in Table 9-1 below. Each column shows the memory during each pass. A stroke (/) in a row indicates a change in that variable during the pass as the program works down through the list. The number of tests (comparisons) made on each pass is also shown in the table. If you don't understand the algorithm, work through the table with the structure plan.

Table 9-1. Computer memory during a bubble sort

Pass:	1	2	3	4
X(1):	27/13	13/ 9	9/ 5	5/ 3
X(2):	13/27/ 9	9/13/ 5	5/ 9/ 3	3/ 5
X(3):	9/27/ 5	5/13/ 3	3/ 9	9
X(4):	5/27/ 3	3/13	13	13
X(5):	3/27	27	27	27
Tests:	4	3	2	1

On the Kth pass there are exactly N–K tests, so the total number of tests is

$1 + 2 + 3 + ... + (N–1) = N(N–1)/2$.

So for a list of five numbers there are 10 tests, but for 10 numbers there are 45 tests. The computer time needed goes up as the square of the length of the list.

Suppose we have less than 1 000 numbers in the list, to be printed in ascending order. Assume, for the purposes of neat printout, that the numbers are all integers less than 100. The program is then:

```
10   REM BUBBLE-SORT
15   DIM X(1000)                'NOT MORE THAN 1000 NUMBERS
20   READ N                     'N <= 1000
30   FOR I = 1 TO N
35     READ X(I)
37   NEXT I
40
50   FOR K = 1 TO N–1           ' N–1 PASSES
60     FOR J = 1 TO N–K         ' N–K COMPARISONS ON KTH PASS
70       IF X(J) > X(J+1) THEN GOSUB 1000
120    NEXT J
130  NEXT K
140
150  FOR I = 1 TO N
155    PRINT USING "####"; X(I);
157  NEXT I
160
170  DATA 10
```

```
 180  DATA 7, 3, 1, 9, 8, 10, 2, 4, 6, 5
 190  END
 200
1000  REM SWOP THEM
1010    T = X(J)
1020    X(J) = X(J+1)
1030    X(J+1) = T
1040  RETURN
```

Microsoft BASIC has a SWAP statement which may be used to exchange the contents of two variables directly. Line 70 can be replaced by

```
70     IF X(J) > X(J+1) THEN SWAP X(J), X(J+1)
```

in which case lines 1000–1040 may be deleted.

9.3.1. Sorting Strings

It would be very useful to be able to sort strings (i.e. words) alphabetically. This can be done easily in BASIC because it has a "lexical collating sequence" such that the string N$ is "less than" the string M$ if N$ is alphabetically ahead of M$. The following program segment reads in two words, and prints them out in alphabetical order:

```
10 READ A$,B$
20 IF A$ < B$ THEN PRINT A$, B$ ELSE PRINT B$, A$
30 DATA CAT, CAR
90 END
```

BASIC uses the ASCII (American Standard Code for Information Interchange) lexical collating sequence, which is set out in full in Appendix F. The sequence is based on the computer's internal binary representation of the character set. So, for example, the following logical expressions are all true:

```
  "A"     < "B"
  " A"    < "A"
  "A "    < "AA"
"MCBEAN" < "McBEAN"
"MC BEAN" < "MCBEAN"
```

Note that the blank precedes "A" in the collating sequence, and that the upper case letters all precede the lower case ones. As an exercise, amend the bubble sort to sort words instead of numbers. In the above program replace every X by X$, and T by T$. Also replace line 155 by

```
155    PRINT X$(I)
```

to print the words on separate lines. The DATA statements must also be changed. Alternatively, INPUT can be used in line 35 instead of READ.

Postscript:

The special functions ASC and CHR$ may be used to get the ASCII code for a character, and vice versa. The following program prints the alphabet on one line in small letters:

```
10   FOR I = 97 TO 122
```

```
20      PRINT CHR$( I );
30      NEXT I
40      PRINT
```

9.4. Order of Merit List

As a variation on the bubble sort, the following program reads a list of N students' names and test marks, and prints them in "order of merit":

```
10    REM ORDER OF MERIT LIST
12    DIM N$(1000)                          'NOT MORE THAN 1000 NAMES
15    DIM X(1000)
20    READ N                                'N <= 1000
30    FOR I = 1 TO N
35      READ N$(I), X(I)
37    NEXT I
40
50    FOR K = 1 TO N-1                      'N-1 PASSES
60      FOR J = 1 TO N-K                    'N-K COMPARISONS ON KTH PASS
70        IF X(J) < X(J+1) THEN GOSUB 1000
120     NEXT J
130   NEXT K
140
150   FOR I = 1 TO N
155     PRINT USING " \              \ "; N$(I);
156     PRINT USING "###"; X(I)
157   NEXT I
160
170   DATA 5
190   DATA ABLE ER, 65
200   DATA BAKER GH, 48
210   DATA CARTER TY, 99
220   DATA HENRY NK, 13
230   DATA JONES RB, 76
980   END
990
1000  REM SWOP THE MARKS
1010    T = X(J)
1020    X(J) = X(J+1)
1030    X(J+1) = T
1040  REM BETTER SWOP THE NAMES TOO!
1050    T$ = N$(J)
1060    N$(J) = N$(J+1)
1070    N$(J+1) = T$
1080  RETURN
```

If you want to use this in a real application, you should be warned that it can chew up an enormous amount of time on a microcomputer. For example, to produce such an order of merit for a class of 200 students on an Apple IIe takes about 20 minutes! An improvement on this method is described by Hahn (1987). This approximately halves the computing time. A further reduction results from using a Quick Sort, and if the code is compiled, instead of interpreted, the same process runs in about 30 seconds.

9.5. Top of the Class

The program in §4.3 to find the student with the highest mark in the class assumes that there is only one such student. We need to use a list if there is likely to be more than one student at the top:

```
10   DIM T$(100)                    ' NOT MORE THAN 100 NAMES
20   READ N                         ' N STUDENTS
30   MAX = -1                       ' MAX IS TOP MARK
40   J = 1                          ' J STUDENTS HAVE TOP MARK
45                                  ' .. THEIR NAMES ARE IN T$
50   FOR I = 1 TO N
60     READ N$, M
70     IF M > MAX THEN GOSUB 1000 ELSE IF M = MAX THEN GOSUB 2000
80   NEXT I
90
100  FOR I = 1 TO J
110    PRINT USING " \          \ "; T$ (I);
115    PRINT USING "####"; MAX
120  NEXT I
130
150  DATA 6
160  DATA JONES, 58
170  DATA SMITH, 72
175  DATA ROGERS, 72
180  DATA JACKSON, 72
190  DATA GREEN, 90
200  DATA MURRAY, 90
210  END
990
1000 REM NEW TOP MARK
1010   MAX = M
1020   J = 1                        ' RESET COUNTER
1030   T$(J) = N$                   ' START NEW LIST
1040 RETURN
1099
2000 REM TIE FOR TOP MARK
2010   J = J + 1                    ' ADVANCE COUNTER
2020   T$(J) = N$                   ' ADD N$ TO LIST
2030 RETURN
```

As an exercise run through the program with the data as given. Note that at the end, the name "JACKSON" will still be in the array T$ (in location 3), but his name will not be printed in line 110, because the "pointer" J has been reset to 2 and will prevent this.

9.6. Updating Student Records Again

In §8.4 we considered how to write students' names to a diskette file, and then how to write one set of marks to the file. However, the program that sends marks to the file (the third one in §8.4) cannot be used exactly as it stands to record the results of a second test, because line 140 now needs to input the student's first test mark as well as his name, and then to write both test marks back to the file (i.e. we don't want to lose his first test mark in the process). One way to solve this problem is to change lines 140, 160 and 170 to read:

```
140     INPUT #1, N$, MK1
160     INPUT MK2
170     WRITE #2, N$, MK1, MK2
```

But then similar changes need to be made again when the third set of marks is to be entered.

A much better solution is to write a general purpose program that uses the first N elements of an array MK(20), say, to read the existing marks from the record file, and then inputs the latest mark into the element MK(N+1) which is written back to the file with all the other marks. This way the same program can be used over and over again to update the student record file. The file will need some extra information though: the number of tests (or offerings) currently in the file. For good measure we may as well also record the maximum mark for each offering in the file so as to be able to do a complete analysis of each offering.

Before we write the general purpose program, the program in §8.4 that writes the names initially to the file (the first program in that section) needs to be amended to record the number of offerings currently in the file (none to start with). The amended initializing program is then:

```
10    REM WRITES NAMES TO FILE
20    OPEN "RECORD" FOR OUTPUT AS #1
25    NOFF = 0                      'NO. OF OFFERINGS IN FILE IS ZERO AT FIRST
27    WRITE #1, NOFF                'IN THE FIRST LINE OF THE FILE
30    INPUT N$
40    WHILE N$ <> "DUMMY"
50       WRITE #1, N$
60       INPUT N$
70    WEND
80    CLOSE #1
90    END
RUN
? ABLE ER
? BAKER IJ
? SMITH ZZ
? DUMMY
Ok
```

If you now examine the file RECORD with the program READ developed in §8.4 you will see that the first line contains a single zero, and that the names are on the subsequent lines. The general purpose program to add any number of offerings (called UPDATE) is then as follows:

```
100   REM READS OLD RECORD AND ADDS NEW OFFERING
110   DIM MAX(20)                   'MAXIMA FOR EACH OFFERING
120   DIM MK(20)                    'EACH STUDENT'S SET OF OFFERINGS
130   OPEN "RECORD" FOR INPUT AS #1
140   OPEN "SCRATCH" FOR OUTPUT AS #2
150                                 '
160   INPUT #1, NOFF                'FIRST GET CURRENT NO. OF OFFERINGS ..
170   FOR I = 1 TO NOFF
180      INPUT #1, MAX(I)           ' ..THEN GET THE MAXIMA
190   NEXT I
200                                 '
210   CLS
```

```
220   INPUT "What is maximum mark for new offering"; MAXNEW
230   MAX( NOFF+1 ) = MAXNEW
240                                   'NOW WRITE NEW NO. OF OFFERINGS AND ..
250                                   ' ..MAXIMA TO FILE
260   PRINT #2, NOFF+1; ",";
270   FOR I = 1 TO NOFF
280     PRINT #2, MAX(I); ",";
290   NEXT I
300   PRINT #2, MAX( NOFF+1 )
310                                   'NOW GET NAMES AND OLD MARKS ...
320   WHILE NOT EOF( 1 )
330     INPUT #1, N$                  ' .. THATS HIS NAME
340     FOR I = 1 TO NOFF
350       INPUT #1, MK(I)             ' .. AND THEMS HIS OLD MARKS
360     NEXT I
370                                   'NOW GET HIS NEW MARK ..
380     PRINT N$; "    ";
390     INPUT MK( NOFF+1 )
400                                   ' ..AND WRITE HIS NAME AND ALL HIS
410                                   ' ..MARKS BACK TO THE FILE!
420     PRINT #2, N$; ",";
430     FOR I = 1 TO NOFF
440       PRINT #2, MK(I); ",";
450     NEXT I
460     PRINT #2, MK( NOFF+1 )
470   WEND
480                                   ,
490   CLOSE #1
500   KILL "RECORD"
510   CLOSE #2
520   NAME "SCRATCH" AS "RECORD"
530   END
SAVE "UPDATE"
RUN
What is maximum mark for new offering?
100
ABLE ER ? 98
BAKER IJ ? 43
SMITH ZZ ? 76
```

Note that PRINT # is used in this program and not WRITE #. This is because WRITE # (and WRITE for that matter) always start a new line of output, unlike PRINT # which enables you to add to the previous line. The use of WRITE # would therefore result in each mark being entered on a new line in the file which is a waste of space. But since PRINT # does not insert commas between items like WRITE # does, these must be inserted as literal constants by PRINT #. Lines 300 and 460 ensure that the next items printed go into a new line in the file.

We now need a second general purpose program (called DISPLAY) to read the file and print the names and marks on the screen:

```
100   REM DISPLAYS STUDENT RECORD FILE
110   DIM MAX(20)                     'MAXIMA
120   DIM MK(20)                      'EACH STUDENT'S MARKS
130   OPEN "RECORD" FOR INPUT AS #1
140                                   ,
```

```
150   INPUT #1, NOFF                          'GET NO. OF OFFERINGS ...
160   FOR I = 1 TO NOFF
170     INPUT #1, MAX(I)                      ' .. AND THEIR MAXIMA
180   NEXT I
190                                           ,
200   CLS
210   FMT$ = " \ " + SPACE$(20) +  " \ "
220   S$ = "####"                             'FORMAT FIELD FOR MARKS
230                                           'PRINT HEADINGS
240   PRINT USING FMT$; "MAX MARK:";
250   FOR I = 1 TO NOFF
260     PRINT USING S$; MAX(I);
270   NEXT I
280   PRINT
290   PRINT
300                                           'NOW FETCH RECORDS AND PRINT THEM
310   WHILE NOT EOF( 1 )
320     INPUT #1, N$
330     PRINT USING FMT$; N$;
340     FOR I = 1 TO NOFF
350       INPUT #1, MK(I)
360       PRINT USING S$; MK(I);
370     NEXT I
380     PRINT
390   WEND
395
400   CLOSE
410   END
SAVE "DISPLAY"
RUN
MAX MARK:        100

ABLE ER           98
BAKER IJ          43
SMITH ZZ          76
```

To add a new offering we now simply run the program UPDATE:

```
RUN "UPDATE"
What is maximum mark for new offering? 25
ABLE ER ? 12
BAKER IJ ? 0
SMITH ZZ ? 23
```

To display the updated record:

```
RUN "DISPLAY"
MAX MARK:        100    25

ABLE ER           98    12
BAKER IJ          43     0
SMITH ZZ          76    23
```

Both programs could in practice be subroutines of a larger "menu driven" program which asks you whether you want to enter a new offering, or display the current record, or whatever. It is fairly straightforward to extend DISPLAY to analyse the results by computing means and standard deviations, and to classify results as first class, second class, etc.

9.7. A Basic Budget

In this section we develop a program to compare monthly budget and expenditure. You should easily be able to adapt it for use at work or at home. The principle is that each month you initially tell the program what categories of expenses you want to have (e.g. household, transport, etc.) and how much you want to budget for each category. This information is stored in a file which is named according to the month in question. Then whenever you incur expenses during that month you simply run the program and for each transaction input a pre-determined (single letter) code for the expense category, and the amount to be debited to that category. When each session is over (indicated by the dummy expense code "@" the program prints the current status of the account.

A variation on the OPEN statement is introduced here:

n   OPEN "FILENAME" FOR APPEND AS #1

APPEND allows additional information to be added on to the end of a file (as opposed to OPEN FOR OUTPUT which erases the current content and starts all over again). File handling can get rather involved, so it is wise to draw up a structure plan before plunging into the code. The general structure plan is:

1. Start up
2. If initializing for a new month then
    2.1. Open file for output
    2.2. Set up expense codes, explanations, budgets, and write them to file
    2.3. Close file
3. Open file for append
4. Unless no more transactions repeat
    4.1. Input expense code, amount (@, 0 to end)
5. Close file
6. Open the file for input
7. Get codes, explanations and budgets from file
8. Unless End-of-File repeat
    8.1. Get expense code and amount, allocate amount to appropriate category and keep running total of expenses
9. Print monthly statement.

The complete program and some sample runs follow:

```
100   REM A BASIC BUDGET
110   DIM BUD(20)       'BUDGET ALLOCATIONS
120   DIM CD$(20)       'BUDGET CODES (SINGLE LETTERS)
130   DIM EXPL$(20)     'EXPLANATIONS OF CODES
140   DIM SPEND(20)     'EXPENDITURE UNDER EACH CODE
150   REM AN$           :ANSWER TO QUESTION
160   REM BD$           :EXPENSE CODE FOR CURRENT TRANSACTION
170   REM I             :GENERAL COUNTER
180   REM MON$          :CURRENT MONTH
190   REM NC            :NUMBER OF CODES
200   REM TOTBUD        :TOTAL BUDGET
210   REM TOTEX         :TOTAL EXPENDITURE
220   REM TRANS         :AMOUNT OF CURRENT TRANSACTION
```

```
230
240   CLS
250   INPUT "MONTH"; MON$
260   INPUT "IS THIS AN INITIALIZATION (Y/N)"; AN$
270   IF AN$ = "Y" THEN GOSUB 1000
280
290   OPEN MON$ FOR APPEND AS #1
300   REM NOW ENTER TRANSACTIONS IN FORM BUDGET CODE,
310   REM AMOUNT. USE CODE OF "@" TO END
320
330   PRINT
340   INPUT "TRANSACTION: ", BD$, TRANS
350   IF BD$ = "@" THEN GOTO 390
360      WRITE #1, BD$, TRANS
370      INPUT "TRANSACTION ": BD$, TRANS
380   GOTO 350
390   CLOSE
400
410   REM NOW READ FILE ... COMPUTE TOTAL EXPENDITURE ...
420   OPEN MON$ FOR INPUT AS #1
430   INPUT #1, NC
440   FOR I = 1 TO NC
450      INPUT #1, CD$(I), EXPL$(I), BUD(I)
460   NEXT I
470
480   WHILE NOT EOF( 1 )
490      INPUT #1, BD$, TRANS
500      FOR I = 1 TO NC
510         IF BD$ = CD$(I) THEN GOSUB 1200
520      NEXT I
530   WEND
540
545   REM ... AND TOTAL BUDGET
550   FOR I = 1 TO NC
625      PRINT
560      TOTBUD = TOTBUD + BUD(I)
570   NEXT I
580
590   REM ... AND PRINT ACCOUNT ANALYSIS
600   CLS
610   PRINT "STATEMENT FOR THE MONTH OF "; MON$
620   PRINT
625   PRINT
630   PRINT TAB(21) "BUDGET" TAB(36) "ACTUAL" TAB(50) "VARIANCE"
640   PRINT
650   FOR I = 1 TO NC
660      PRINT EXPL$(I) TAB(20);
670      PRINT USING "####.##"; BUD(I);
680      PRINT TAB(35)
690      PRINT USING "####.##"; SPEND(I);
700      PRINT TAB(50)
710      PRINT USING "####.##+"; BUD(I) − SPEND(I)
720   NEXT I
730
740   PRINT
750   PRINT "TOTAL:" TAB(20);
760   PRINT USING "####.##"; TOTBUD;
```

```
770   PRINT TAB(35)
780   PRINT USING "####.##"; TOTEX;
790   PRINT TAB(50)
800   PRINT USING "####.##+"; TOTBUD − TOTEX
810   END
820
1000  REM INITIALIZATION: SET UP CODES, EXPLANATIONS, BUDGETS,
1010  REM AND WRITE THEM TO THE FILE MON$
1020  PRINT
1030  INPUT "HOW MANY CODES"; NC
1040  OPEN MON$ FOR OUTPUT AS #1
1050  WRITE #1, NC
1060  FOR I = 1 TO NC
1070    PRINT USING "CODE ##:"; i;
1080    INPUT; " ", CD$(I)
1090    CD$(I) = LEFT$( CD$(I), 1 )                              'JUST IN CASE!
1100    INPUT; "  EXPLANATION: ", EXPL$(I)
1105    PRINT TAB(45)
1110    INPUT "  BUDGET: ", BUD(I)
1120    WRITE #1, CD$(I), EXPL$(I), BUD(I)
1130  NEXT I
1140  CLOSE
1150  RETURN
1160
1200  REM ALLOCATE EXPENDITURE AND KEEP RUNNING TOTAL
1210  SPEND(I) = SPEND(I) + TRANS
1220  TOTEX = TOTEX + TRANS
1230  RETURN
```

Some sample runs are as follows.

```
RUN
MONTH? MAY
IS THIS AN INITIALIZATION (Y/N)? Y

HOW MANY CODES? 5
CODE 1: C    EXPLANATION: CLOTHING          BUDGET: 75
CODE 2: E    EXPLANATION: ENTERTAINMENT     BUDGET: 50
CODE 3: H    EXPLANATION: HOUSEHOLD         BUDGET: 500
CODE 4: R    EXPLANATION: REST              BUDGET: 300
CODE 5: T    EXPLANATION: TRANSPORT         BUDGET: 80

TRANSACTION: H, 120
TRANSACTION: T, 20
TRANSACTION: C, 25
TRANSACTION: E, 12.50
TRANSACTION: @, 0
```

STATEMENT FOR THE MONTH OF MAY

	BUDGET	ACTUAL	VARIANCE
CLOTHING	75.00	25.00	50.00+
ENTERTAINMENT	50.00	12.50	37.50+
HOUSEHOLD	500.00	120.00	380.00+
REST	300.00	0.00	300.00+
TRANSPORT	80.00	20.00	60.00+
TOTAL:	1005.00	177.50	827.50+

```
Ok
RUN
MONTH? MAY
IS THIS AN INITIALIZATION (Y/N)? N

TRANSACTION: E, 50
TRANSACTION: C, 79.99
TRANSACTION: R, 29.82
TRANSACTION: @, 0

STATEMENT FOR THE MONTH OF MAY
```

	BUDGET	ACTUAL	VARIANCE
CLOTHING	75.00	104.99	29.99−
ENTERTAINMENT	50.00	62.50	12.50−
HOUSEHOLD	500.00	120.00	380.00+
REST	300.00	29.82	270.18+
TRANSPORT	80.00	20.00	60.00+
TOTAL:	1005.00	337.31	667.69+

Note that a file must be CLOSEd before it can be OPENed again. The statement

n   CLOSE #m

closes file #m. If #m is omitted, all files are closed.

The string function LEFT$ is used in line 1090 to capture the leftmost character of the expense code in case more than one letter was used. This and other useful string functions are described in Appendix E.

9.8. Postscript

The files used in all the examples so far are "sequential" files because they are read and written in the same order always: from beginning to end. They can be rather time consuming since if, for example, you wanted to get information near the end of a file, it has to be read right from the beginning. So if you want to use files in a real application you may want to consider "random access" files, which are much quicker to handle, but require more programming. As such they are beyond the scope of this book, but you should be able to find out about them from your computer manual.

REFERENCE

Cooke D., Craven A.H. and Clarke G.M. *Basic Statistical Computing*, Edward Arnold, London, 1982.

Hahn B.D. *Problem Solving with FORTRAN 77*, Edward Arnold, London, 1987.

9.9. EXERCISES

9.1 If NUM is a BASIC array write the lines of coding which will
   (a) put the first 100 non-negative integers (0, ..., 99) in the elements NUM(0), ..., NUM(99);
   (b) put the first 50 positive even integers (2, ..., 100) in the elements NUM(1), ..., NUM(50).

9.2 Write a program which will read in a number (assumed less than 31, say) and print its binary representation on one line with no blanks between the digits.

9.3 Write a program which puts the first 100 Fibonacci numbers (1, 1, 2, 3, 5, 8, ...) into an array F(1), ..., F(100).

9.4 A prime number is one which is exactly divisible only by itself and unity. Develop a structure plan for the problem of printing all the primes less than 1000 (1 and 2 are generally regarded as primes, and will probably have to be dealt with separately). Hints: (1) use an array to store the primes; (2) to save computer time use the fact that if a number has no factors less than its square root, then it has none greater than its square root.

9.5 Write the program for Ex. 9.4.

9.6 A formula, called Zeller's Congruence, may be used to compute the day of the week given the date (within a certain range of dates). The formula is

$$f = ([2.6m - 0.2] + k + y + [y/4] + [c/4] - 2c) \text{ modulo } 7,$$

where the square brackets mean "the integer part of", modulo means "remainder when divided by", and

m = month number, with January and February taken as months 11 and 12 of the preceding year, so March is then month 1, and December month 10;

k = day of the month;

c = first two digits of the year (i.e. the century number);

y = year in the century.

E.g., 23rd August 1963 has $m = 6$, $k = 23$, $c = 19$, $y = 63$;
 1st January 1800 has $m = 11$, $k = 1$, $c = 17$, $y = 99$.

Write a program to read the date in the usual form (e.g. 31 01 1863 for 31st January 1863) and print out the given date and the day of the week (in words) on which it falls. Hint: use a string array for the days of the week. Test your program on some known dates, like today's date, or 7th December 1941 (Pearl Harbour Sunday).

The formula will not work if you go too far back. Shakespeare and Cervantes both died on 23rd April 1616. Shakespeare died on a Tuesday, but Cervantes died on a Saturday! This is because England had not yet adopted the Gregorian calendar and were consequently 10 days behind the rest of the world.

10 SIMULATION

One of the most powerful applications of modern computers is in simulation — running a "computer experiment" which mirrors some aspect of the real world under study. A large class of interesting problems in reality are influenced by "random" effects (randomness is often simply a measure of our ignorance of what is really going on). Random events are easily simulated in BASIC with the function RND. This is a pseudo-random number generator which returns a uniformly distributed pseudo-random number in the open interval (0, 1). E.g.

```
10   FOR I = 1 TO 10
20      PRINT RND
30   NEXT I
RUN
 .7151002
 .683111
 .4821425
 .9992938
 .6465093
```

10.1. Rolling a Fair Die

As an example, let us write a program to simulate 20 rolls of a fair (unbiased) six-sided die:

```
10   FOR I = 1 TO 20
20      PRINT INT( 6 * RND + 1 );
30   NEXT I
40   END
```

The resulting output is:

4 3 4 6 2 5 5 1 2 6 2 3 6 1 3 3 4 2 3 2

Since RND is a decimal number in the range (0; 1), 6*RND will be in the range (0; 6), and 6*RND+1 will be in the range (1; 7) exclusive, i.e. between 1.00001 and 6.99999. Therefore the integer part of 6*RND+1 (line 20 in the program) will give the required result: a random integer between 1 and 6 inclusive.

However, re-running this program always gives the same sequence of results, which is not true to life, as every gambler knows! This is because the random number sequence is always started at the same place in the above program. This is easily remedied by the function RANDOMIZE, which sets the starting point for RND, or "seeds" it. Since the computer has an inbuilt timer, RANDOMIZE should be used in conjunction with the function TIMER, which returns the number of seconds elapsed since midnight. Since this is very likely to be different each time the program is run, the same program will produce DIFFERENT output every time as follows:

```
10   RANDOMIZE TIMER
20   FOR I = 1 TO 20
30     PRINT INT( 6 * RND + 1);
40   NEXT I
50   END
```

The output (when the program is run at 52716.77 seconds past midnight) is:

6 6 5 1 4 1 4 6 4 1 4 2 6 5 1 2 1 3 2 1

We can therefore simulate any number of experiments involving rolling dice. This may be quicker and cheaper than doing real experiments. We can even do some statistics on our simulated experiments, just as if they were real. For example, we could find the mean of the number on the uppermost face of the die, when it is rolled 100 times, and also the probability of getting a six:

```
10   RANDOMIZE TIMER
15   T = 0
17   N6 = 0
20   FOR I = 1 TO 100
30     N = INT( 6 * RND + 1)
40     T = T + N
50     IF N = 6 THEN N6 = N6 + 1
60   NEXT I
70   PRINT USING "MEAN: #.##"; T / 100
80   PRINT USING "PROB OF SIX: #.##"; N6 / 100
90   END
```

Sample output from two different runs:

MEAN: 3.67
PROB OF SIX: 0.16
MEAN: 3.41
PROB OF SIX: 0.16

10.2. Simulating Bacteria Division

When a die is rolled, each face lands uppermost with equal probability, which is why a statement such as the one in line 30 above may be used in the simulation. But if the probabilities of the various events are not equally likely, a slightly different approach is needed. Suppose, for example, that a certain type of bacteria divides (into two) in a given time interval with a probability of 0.75 (75%), and that if it does not divide, it dies. Since RND produces a random number which is uniformly distributed, it is equally likely to lie anywhere on the real line between 0 and 1. The chances of it being less than 0.75 are therefore precisely 75%, which enables us to simulate this situation as follows:

```
10   RANDOMIZE TIMER
20   R = RND
30   IF R <= 0.75 THEN PRINT "I AM NOW WE"
40   IF R > 0.75 THEN PRINT "I AM NO MORE"
50   END
```

Why would the following be wrong?

```
30  IF RND <= 0.75 THEN PRINT "I AM NOW WE"
40  IF RND > 0.75 THEN PRINT "I AM NO MORE"
```

10.3. Spinning a Fair Coin

The next program simulates 50 spins of a fair coin.

```
10  RANDOMIZE TIMER
20  FOR I = 1 TO 50
30     IF RND < 0.5 THEN PRINT "H"; ELSE PRINT "T";
40  NEXT I
50  END
```

Sample output from two different runs:

HHHHTHTTTTHTHTTTTTHTHHHTTTTHHTHHTTHHHHHHTHHTTTTTTH
HHHTTHTTTHTTTHHTHHHTTHHTTHHTHHTTTTTTHTTHTHHHHHHTHT

Note that there is no way of telling whether these are the results of a real or simulated experiment. This is what simulation is all about.

10.4. A Random Walk

Suppose a drunken sailor has to negotiate a jetty toward his ship. The jetty is 50 steps long and 20 wide. A mate places him in the middle of the jetty at the quay end, and points him toward the ship. Suppose at every step he has a 60% chance of lurching toward the ship, but a 20% chance of lurching to the left or right (he manages to be always facing the ship). If he reaches the ship end of the jetty he is hauled aboard by waiting mates. The problem is to simulate his progress along the jetty, and to estimate his chances of getting to the ship without falling into the sea. To do this correctly, we must simulate one "walk" along the jetty, ascertain whether or not he reaches the ship, and then repeat this simulation 1000 times, say. The proportion of simulations that end with the sailor safely in the ship will be an estimate of his chances of making it to the ship. For a given walk we assume that if he has not either reached the ship or fallen into the sea after, say, 10000 steps, he dies of thirst on the jetty.

To represent the jetty, we set up an X,Y co-ordinate system (where X and Y are measured in steps) with the X-axis running along the middle of the jetty from the quay to the ship, with the origin at the quay end. So the sailor starts his walk from the origin. The structure plan and program for this problem are as follows:

1. Initialize variables
2. Repeat 1000 simulated walks down the jetty
    2.1. Start at the land end of the jetty
    2.2. While not in the sea AND still alive repeat:
        2.2.1. Get a random number
        2.2.2. If $r < 0.6$ then
            2.2.2.1. Move forward (shipward)
        2.2.3. If $r < 0.8$ and $r \geq 0.6$ then
            2.2.3.1. Move port (left)
        2.2.4. If $r \geq 0.8$ then
            2.2.4.1. Move starboard (right)

2.2.5. Increase step counter
2.3. If he got to the ship then
2.3.1. Increase safe home counter
3. Compute and print probability of reaching ship.

The program goes like this:

```
100  REM RANDOM WALK
110  RANDOMIZE TIMER
120  H = 0                          ' NO. OF TIMES HE MAKES IT
130  S = 1000                       ' NO. OF SIMULATED WALKS
140
150  FOR I = 1 TO S
160     X = 0                       ' START AT ORIGIN EACH TIME
170     Y = 0
180     N = 0                       ' NO. OF STEPS ON A GIVEN WALK
190
200     WHILE X <= 50 AND ABS( Y ) <= 10 AND N <= 10000
210        R = RND
220        IF R < 0.6 THEN X = X + 1
230        IF R < 0.8 AND R >= 0.6 THEN Y = Y + 1
240        IF R >= 0.8 THEN Y = Y - 1
250        N = N + 1
260     WEND
270
280     REM DID HE ACTUALLY MAKE IT?
290     IF X > 50 THEN H = H + 1
310  NEXT I
315
320  PRINT USING "PROB OF REACHING SHIP:###.##"; H / S
330  END
```

10.5. Traffic Flow

A major use of simulation in large cities is to model the traffic flow, so as to be able to try out different traffic light patterns on the computer before imposing them on the real traffic. (This has been done on a large scale in Leeds in the U.K.) In this example we look at a small part of this problem: how to simulate the flow of a single line of traffic through one set of traffic lights. We make the following assumptions (which can be changed, of course):

1) Traffic travels straight, without turning.

2) The probability of a car arriving at the lights in any one second is independent of what happened during the previous second. This is called a Poisson process. This probability (call it p) may be estimated by watching cars at the intersection and monitoring their arrival pattern. In this simulation, we take p = 0.3 (this is entirely arbitrary).

3) When the lights are green, assume the cars move through at a steady rate of, say, 8 every 10 seconds (this can also be estimated in reality).

4) In this simulation, we will take the basic time interval to be 10 seconds, so we want a printout showing the length of the queue (if any) of traffic at the lights every 10 seconds.

SIMULATION

5) We will set the lights red or green for variable multiples of 10 seconds.

The complete program is as follows:

```
010   REM TRAFFIC FLOW SIMULATION
020   REM INTERVALS ARE 10 SECONDS
030   RANDOMIZE TIMER
040   CLS
050   INPUT R, G, T           'RED FOR R*10-SECS, GREEN FOR G *10-SECS
060   P = 0.3                 'PROB A CAR ARRIVES IN GIVEN SECOND
070   R1 = 0                  'RED TIMER
080   G1 = 0                  'GREEN TIMER
090   C = 0                   'NO CARS TO START WITH
100   L$ = "R"                'LIGHTS RED TO START WITH
105
110   FOR I = 1 TO T          'RUN FOR T 10-SEC INTERVALS
120      FOR J = 1 TO 10
130         IF RND < P THEN C = C + 1      'FIND HOW MANY CARS ARRIVE
140      NEXT J
150      IF L$ = "G" THEN GOSUB 300 ELSE GOSUB 500
160   NEXT I
220   END
225
300   REM LIGHTS GREEN HERE
305      G1 = G1 + 1
310      C = C - 8                         'LET 8 CARS THROUGH
320      IF C < 0 THEN C = 0               'MAY HAVE BEEN LESS THAN 8!
340      GOSUB 700                         'PRINT TRAFFIC QUEUE
350      IF G1 = G THEN GOSUB 800          'LIGHTS DON'T CHANGE YET
380   RETURN
390
500   REM LIGHTS RED HERE
510      R1 = R1 + 1
520      GOSUB 700
530      IF R1 = R THEN GOSUB 900
560   RETURN
570
700   REM PRINT LINE OF CARS HERE
705      PRINT USING "##"; I;
710      PRINT TAB(5) L$ TAB(10)
720      FOR K = 1 TO C
722         PRINT "*";
724      NEXT K
730      PRINT
740   RETURN
750
800   REM CHANGE FROM GREEN TO RED
810      L$ = "R"
820      G1 = 0
830   RETURN
```

840
900   REM CHANGE FROM RED TO GREEN
910   L$ = "G"
920   R1 = 0
930   RETURN

Sample output (with data 4, 2, 54 for line 50) is as follows:

```
 1   R **
 2   R ******
 3   R **********
 4   R ************
 5   G ****
 6   G
 7   R ******
 8   R ************
 9   R **************
10   R ****************
11   G *************
12   G ******
13   R *********
14   R ************
15   R *************
16   R *****************
17   G **********
18   G ******
19   R ************
20   R ***************
21   R *******************
22   R ***************************
23   G ********************
24   G **************
25   R ****************
26   R *****************
27   R *********************
28   R ***********************
29   G ****************
30   G ***********
31   R *************
32   R *****************
33   R ********************
34   R **********************
35   G ******************
36   G ************
37   R **************
38   R ******************
39   R **********************
40   R *****************************
41   G **************************
42   G ********************
43   R *********************
44   R ************************
45   R **************************
46   R *****************************
47   G ************************
```

```
48  G *******************
49  R ********************
50  R ***********************
51  R **************************
52  R *****************************
53  G ************************
54  G *******************
```

From this particular run it seems that a traffic jam is building up, although more and longer runs of the simulation are needed to see if this is really the case. In that case, one can experiment with different periods for red and green lights in order to get an acceptable traffic pattern before setting the real lights to that particular cycle. This is the great value of this sort of simulation. Of course we can get even closer to reality by considering two way traffic, and allowing cars to turn in both directions, but the above program gives the basic ideas.

10.6. Dealing a Bridge Hand

Simulation is the basis of most computer games. The next program, which is similar to one by Kemeny and Kurtz (1967), simulates a deal of 13 cards from a pack of 52 playing cards (the jokers have been removed). The names of the four suits are read as strings into the elements 0 to 3 of the array S$, and the 13 face values from TWO to ACE are read into the elements 0 to 12 of the array V$. To deal a card, a random number in the range 0 to 51 is generated, i.e. the 52 cards are represented uniquely by the numbers 0 to 51. The main problem is that a given card may only be dealt once. To ensure this, an array L is set up, with all its elements initially zero (meaning no cards have been dealt yet). When a random number I (line 2010 below) comes up, L(I) is checked. If it is still zero, that card has not been dealt, so I is put into the next element of H (line 70 below), and L(I) is set to -1, indicating that card I has been dealt now. If L(I) already has the value -1 when I comes up, it means that card I has already been dealt, so another random number is generated. This process is repeated 13 times, until the array H contains 13 unique numbers in the range 0 to 51. This part of the problem may be structure planned as follows:

> Repeat 13 times:
> 1. Get a random number RND
> 2. Convert it to an integer I in the range 0 to 51
> 3. While L(I) <> 0 repeat:
>   3.1. Get another random integer I
> 4. Set L(I) to -1
> 5. Assign I to the next element of H.

To print the hand of 13 cards, each element of H is subjected to integer division by 13 (line 3010). The quotient S will be in the range 0 to 3 (won't it?) and gives the suit. The remainder V (line 3020) will be in the range 0 to 12, and gives the face value. E.g. the number 50 on division by 13 gives a quotient of 3 (SPADES) and a remainder of 11 (KING), as shown in the first line of output after the program, which follows:

```
0010  REM SIMULATED DEALING OF A BRIDGE HAND
0020  RANDOMIZE TIMER
0030  DIM H(13)                    'FOR THE 13 CARDS
0032  DIM L(51)                    'THE CHECK LIST
```

```
0034   DIM S$(3)                              'FOR THE SUIT NAMES
0036   DIM V$(12)                             'FOR THE FACE VALUES
0040   GOSUB 1000                             'SET UP THE CARD DECK
0045
0050   FOR C = 1 TO 13
0060     GOSUB 2000                           'DEAL CARD NO. I
0070     H(C) = I                             'PUT IT IN H(C)
0080   NEXT C
0085
0100   REM USE BUBBLE-SORT TO SORT HAND IN DECREASING ORDER
0110   FOR J = 1 TO 13
0120     FOR K = 1 TO 13−J
0130       IF H(K) < H(K+1) THEN SWAP H(K), H(K+1)
0170     NEXT K
0180   NEXT J
0185
0200   REM PRINT THE HAND
0210   FOR C = 1 TO 13
0220     I = H(C)
0230     GOSUB 3000
0240   NEXT C
0250   END
0990
1000   REM SET UP THE DECK HERE
1010     FOR S = 0 TO 3                      'READ NAMES OF SUITS
1012       READ S$(S)
1014     NEXT S
1016
1020     FOR V = 0 TO 12                     'READ FACE VALUES
1022       READ V$(V)
1024     NEXT V
1030     DATA CLUBS, DIAMONDS, HEARTS, SPADES
1040     DATA TWO, THREE, FOUR, FIVE, SIX, SEVEN, EIGHT, NINE, TEN
1050     DATA JACK, QUEEN, KING, ACE
1060   RETURN
1070
2000   REM DEAL A CARD
2010     I = INT( 52 * RND )                 'CARD NO. 0 - 51
2015
2020     WHILE L(I) <> 0                     'NOT DEALT YET
2030       I = INT( 52 * RND )               'TRY AGAIN
2040     WEND
2045
2050     L(I) = −1                           'DEALT NOW
2060   RETURN
2070
3000   REM PRINT CARD NO. I
3010     S = INT( I / 13 )                   'FINDS ITS SUIT
3020     V = I − 13 * S                      'FINDS ITS FACE VALUE
3030     PRINT USING " \      \ "; V$(V);
3040     PRINT " OF ";
3050     PRINT USING " \      \ "; S$(S);
3055     PRINT USING "#####"; H(C), S, V
3060   RETURN
```

A different hand will be dealt every time the program is run. Here is a sample hand (the headings for the last three columns have been inserted into the text for clarity):

	H(C)	S	V
KING OF SPADES	50	3	11
SIX OF SPADES	43	3	4
FIVE OF SPADES	42	3	3
FIVE OF HEARTS	29	2	3
FOUR OF HEARTS	28	2	2
THREE OF HEARTS	27	2	1
SEVEN OF DIAMONDS	18	1	5
SIX OF DIAMONDS	17	1	4
FIVE OF DIAMONDS	16	1	3
FOUR OF DIAMONDS	15	1	2
ACE OF CLUBS	12	0	12
QUEEN OF CLUBS	10	0	10
SEVEN OF CLUBS	5	0	5

You may think that the method of "shuffling" the cards, with the WHILE-WEND loop in lines 2020 to 2040 is inefficient, because as more cards get dealt, so the number of invocations of RND goes up and up. The following alterations to the program shuffles all 52 cards in the pack by starting with a sorted pack and swopping them at random, rather like a bubble sort.

```
0030    DIM H(52)
.
0041    FOR I = 1 TO 52
0042       H(I) = I – 1
0043    NEXT I
.
0050    FOR C = 1 TO 52
.
0070                             ' DELETE LINE 70
.
2000    REM DEAL A CARD
2010    R = INT( 52 * RND ) + 1
2020    SWAP H(R), H(C)          'DELETE LINES 2030–2050
2060    RETURN
```

Note that R (line 2010) is now in the range 1 to 52 since it represents the position of a card rather than the card itself. With a few more amendments all four hands can be printed. You may like to compare the computing time used by the two methods by printing the value of TIMER at the start and end of each program.

10.7. Queues

In this section we look at how to simulate a simple first-in first-out (FIFO) queue. There are TWO random processes involved: the arrival of users, and the service of users, both of which we assume to be Poisson distributed. These processes may be represented by two random variables: the inter-arrival time *(IAT)* between users joining the end of the queue, and the service time *(ST)* for the user at the front of the queue. Let us suppose that these random variables are distributed as follows (they could be the result of a survey in a Post Office):

IAT (secs)	Prob (frequency)	Prob (cumulative)
10	0.10	0.10
15	0.25	0.35
20	0.30	0.65
25	0.25	0.90
30	0.10	1.00

ST (secs)	Prob (frequency)	Prob (cumulative)
5	0.08	0.08
10	0.14	0.22
15	0.18	0.40
20	0.24	0.64
25	0.22	0.86
30	0.14	1.00

In the program below, variables have been defined as follows:

A: clock time of arrival
E: clock time of entry into service
I: inter-arrival time (random)
L: clock time of leaving service
S: service time (random) (L = E + S)
T: user's time in system (T = L − A)
W: user's wait time (W = E − A).

The purpose of the simulation is to generate mean time in the system and mean wait time, to see if these are acceptable. The structure plan is as follows:

1. Repeat for each user
    1.1. Generate I according to Poisson distribution
    1.2. Compute arrival time: A = A + I
    1.3. Determine when user enters service as follows:
        If he arrives after previous user has left then
        1.3.1. He enters service immediately (E = A)
        Else
        1.3.2. He waits until previous user leaves (E = L)
    1.4. Generate S according to Poisson distribution
    1.5. Determine when he leaves service: L = E + S
    1.6. Add wait time and time in system to running total

2. Compute mean wait time and mean time in system for all users.

The program simulates the service of 50 users in a FIFO queue, and prints out the variables defined above for each user:

```
100  REM SIMULATION OF A FIFO QUEUE
110  RANDOMIZE TIMER
120  CLS
130  PRINT "     USER    IAT    A    E    S    L    W    T"
140  PRINT
150  A = 0              'CLOCK ARRIVAL TIME
160  E = 0              'CLOCK TIME ENTERING SERVICE
```

```
170    L = 0                  'CLOCK TIME LEAVING SERVICE
180    MWT = 0                'MEAN USER WAIT TIME
190    MTIS = 0               'MEAN USER TIME IN SYSTEM
200    N = 50                 'NUMBER OF USERS
210
220    FOR U = 1 TO N
225
227       REM GENERATE RANDOM I
230       R = RND
240       IF R < 0.1 THEN I = 10
250       IF R >= 0.10 AND R < 0.35 THEN I = 15
260       IF R >= 0.35 AND R < 0.65 THEN I = 20
270       IF R >= 0.65 AND R < 0.90 THEN I = 25
280       IF R >= 0.90 THEN I = 30
290
300       A = A + I
310       IF A >= L THEN E = A ELSE E = L
315
320       REM GENERATE SERVICE TIME S
330       R = RND
340       IF R < 0.08 THEN S = 5
350       IF R >= 0.08 AND R < 0.22 THEN S = 10
360       IF R >= 0.22 AND R < 0.40 THEN S = 15
370       IF R >= 0.40 AND R < 0.64 THEN S = 20
380       IF R >= 0.64 AND R < 0.86 THEN S = 25
390       IF R >= 0.86 THEN S = 30
400
410       L = E + S
420       W = E - A
430       T = L - A
440       MWT = MWT + W
450       MTIS = MTIS + T
460       PRINT USING "######"; U, I, A, E, S, L, W, T
470    NEXT U
480
490    PRINT
500    PRINT USING "MEAN WAIT TIME:   ###.# SECS"; MWT / N
510    PRINT USING "MEAN TIME IN SYSTEM: ###.# SECS"; MTIS / N
520    END
```

Incidentally, in order to get the output neatly under the column headings, it is much easier to get the tables right first, and to put the headings in afterwards to match the columns of output!

Output from a sample run is as follows:

USER	IAT	A	E	S	L	W	T
1	25	25	25	25	50	0	25
2	10	35	50	20	70	15	35
3	15	50	70	30	100	20	50
4	25	75	100	20	120	25	45
5	20	95	120	20	140	25	45
6	20	115	140	5	145	25	30
7	25	140	145	20	165	5	25
8	20	160	165	20	185	5	25
9	15	175	185	10	195	10	20

11	25	220	220	10	230	0	10
12	25	245	245	5	250	0	5
13	15	260	260	10	270	0	10
14	30	290	290	25	315	0	25
15	30	320	320	25	345	0	25
16	30	350	350	10	360	0	10
17	15	365	365	25	390	0	25
18	10	375	390	15	405	15	30
19	10	385	405	25	430	20	45
20	10	395	430	25	455	35	60
21	20	415	455	10	465	40	50
22	25	440	465	20	485	25	45
23	20	460	485	30	515	25	55
24	15	475	515	15	530	40	55
25	20	495	530	25	555	35	60
26	15	510	555	20	575	45	65
27	10	520	575	15	590	55	70
28	25	545	590	25	615	45	70
29	10	555	615	30	645	60	90
30	15	570	645	20	665	75	95
31	25	595	665	15	680	70	85
32	10	605	680	20	700	75	95
33	10	615	700	30	730	85	115
34	15	630	730	20	750	100	120
35	15	645	750	20	770	105	125
36	20	665	770	20	790	105	125
37	15	680	790	25	815	110	135
38	10	690	815	30	845	125	155
39	25	715	845	20	865	130	150
40	25	740	865	30	895	125	155
41	20	760	895	30	925	135	165
42	25	785	925	30	955	140	170
43	10	795	955	30	985	160	190
44	15	810	985	20	1005	175	195
45	15	825	1005	20	1025	180	200
46	20	845	1025	25	1050	180	205
47	20	865	1050	15	1065	185	200
48	15	880	1065	10	1075	185	195
49	20	900	1075	5	1080	175	180
50	20	920	1080	25	1105	160	185

```
MEAN WAIT TIME:         67.0 SECS
MEAN TIME IN SYSTEM:    87.3 SECS
```

10.8. EXERCISES

10.1 Extend the card dealing example of §10.6 to deal all four hands of cards, and to sort each hand before printing. Hint: use the second method outlined in that example to shuffle all 52 cards, and then copy each hand into another array for sorting in a Bubble Sort subroutine.

10.2 In a game of BINGO the numbers 1 to 99 are drawn at random from a bag. Write a program to simulate the draw of the numbers (each number can only be drawn once), printing the drawn numbers ten to a line.

10.3 RND can be used to estimate π as follows. Write a program which generates random points in a square of side two, say, and which counts what proportion of these points fall inside the circle of unit radius that fits exactly into the square. This proportion will be the ratio of the area of the circle to that of the square. Hence estimate π. (This is not a very efficient way to compute π!)

10.4 The aim of this exercise is to simulate bacteria growth. Suppose that a certain type of bacterium divides or dies according to the following assumptions: (1) during a fixed time interval, called a generation, a single bacterium divides into two identical replicas with probability p; (2) if it does NOT divide during that interval, it dies (ceases to be); (3) the offspring (called daughters) will divide or die during the next generation, independently of the past history (there may well be no offspring, in which case the colony becomes extinct). Start with a single individual and write a program which simulates a number of generations. Take $p = 0.75$. The number of generations which you can simulate will depend on your computer system. Carry out a large number (e.g. 100) of such simulations. The probability of ultimate extinction, $p(E)$, may be estimated as the fraction of simulations that end in extinction. You can also estimate the mean size of the nth generation from a large number of simulations (theory says that it should be $(2p)^n$.

Statistical theory asserts that the expected value of the extinction probability $p(E)$ is whichever is the smaller of unity, and $(1-p)/p$. So for $p = 0.75$, $p(E)$ is expected to be 1/3. But for $p \leq 0.5$, $p(E)$ is expected to be unity, which means that extinction is certain (a rather unexpected result). You can use your program to test this theory by running it for different values of p, and estimating $p(E)$ in each case.

10.5 Dribblefire Jets Inc. (Kass, 1977) make two types of aeroplane, the two-engined DFII, and the four engined DFIV. The engines are terrible and fail with probability 0.5 on a standard flight (the engines fail independently of each other). The manufacturers claim that the planes can fly if at least half of their engines are working, i.e. the DFII will crash only if both its engines fail, while the DFIV will crash if all four, or if any three engines fail.

You have been commissioned by the Civil Aviation Bureau to ascertain which of the two models is less likely to crash. Since parachutes are expensive, the cheapest (and safest!) way to do this is to simulate a large number of flights of each model. For example, two calls of RND could represent one standard flight of the DFII: if both random numbers are less than 0.5 then that plane crashes, otherwise it doesn't. Write a program which simulates a large number of flights of both models, and estimate the probability of a crash in each case. If you can run enough simulations, you should get a rather unexpected result. (Incidentally, the probability of n engines failing on a given flight is given by the binomial distribution, but you do not need to use this fact in the program.)

REFERENCES

Kass G.V. Pre-University School, University of the Witwatersrand, Johannesburg, 1977 (unpublished).

Kemeny J.G. and Kurtz T.E. *BASIC Programming*, Wiley, New York, 1967.

11 USER DEFINED FUNCTIONS

BASIC has inbuilt functions, like SIN, COS, SQR, etc, which we have already seen in Chapter Six. We may however wish to define our own functions for use in particular programs.

11.1. The DEF FN Statement

Suppose we need to compute the secant of an angle repeatedly in a program. We can define our own secant function as follows:

```
10   DEF FNSEC( T ) = 1 / COS( T )
     .
     .
40   X = 0.5
50   Y = FNSEC( X )                    ' COMPUTES SEC(0.5)
     .
     .
70   FOR X = 0 TO 1 STEP 0.1           ' PRINTS TABLE
75      PRINT X; FNSEC( X )
80   NEXT X
90   END
```

Note:

1. DEF FN defines the function following on the same line. This definition should be at the start of the program.
2. The function name must be constructed from a valid variable name prefixed with the letters FN. The type (numeric or string) of the value returned by the function is determined in the usual way by the variable name following the letters FN.
3. The function is invoked by mentioning its name anywhere that a BASIC expression may be validly used (e.g. assignment, PRINT, IF, etc.).
4. The arguments (or parameters) following the function name in the DEF statement (T in the above example) are "dummy variables", in that they are used only for the function definition. Variables with the same name in the program will have no connection with such dummy variables.
5. Functions in BASIC may be recursive, that is they may call themselves (this also applies to subroutines). Probably the most notorious example of recursion is Ackermann's function, which is defined as follows:

   $A(0, N) = N + 1$
   $A(M, 0) = A(M-1, 1)$
   $A(M, N) = A(M-1, A(M, N-1))$

   If you tried to compute this in BASIC even for quite small values of M and N (less than about 6) you would soon run out of computer memory, even on a mainframe!

11.2. Example: Newton's Method Again

Newton's method (which is described more fully in Chapter 14) may be used to solve a general equation $f(x) = 0$ by repeating the calculation

x becomes $x - f(x)/f'(x)$

(where $f'(x)$ is the first derivative of $f(x)$) until $f(x)$ has become close enough to zero (check the formula for the square root of a in §5.6 using $f(x) = x^2 - a$).

Suppose $f(x) = x^3 + x - 3$.
Then $f'(x) = 3x^2 + 1$.

Use Newton's method to solve $f(x) = 0$. Start at $x = 2$, and stop when the absolute value of $f(x)$ is less than 0.000001, or after 20 iterations, say.

The program to carry out Newton's method uses two functions: FNF for $f(x)$ and FNDF for $f'(x)$:

```
100  DEF FNF( X ) = X ^ 3 + X - 3
110  DEF FNDF( X ) = 3 * X ^ 2 + 1
130  X = 2                    'STARTING GUESS
140  ITS = 0                  'ITERATION COUNTER
150  MAX = 20                 'MAXIMUM ITERATIONS
160  EPS = 1E-6               'MAXIMUM ERROR
170                           '
180  WHILE ABS( FNF( X ) ) >= EPS AND ITS < MAX
190    X = X - FNF( X ) / FNDF( X )
200    PRINT USING "###.######"; X;
210    PRINT USING "  #.###### ^^^^"; FNF( X )
220    ITS = ITS + 1
240  WEND

250                           '
260  PRINT
270  IF ABS( FNF(X) ) < EPS THEN PRINT "CONVERGED" ELSE PRINT "DIVERGED"
280  END
RUN
1.461538    0.158352E+01
1.247788    0.190564E+00
1.214185    0.418878E-02
1.213412    0.214577E-05
1.213412   -.476837E-06
```

Note that there are two conditions which will stop the loop in lines 180 to 240: either convergence, or the completion of a certain number of iterations.

11.3. EXERCISE

11.1   Write a program which uses the Newton quotient

$[f(x + h) - f(x)] / h$

to estimate the first derivative of $f(x) = x^3$ at $x = 1$, using successively smaller values of h: 1, 1/2, 1/4, 1/8, ...

12 SPECIAL TEXT AND GRAPHICS FACILITIES

A feature of Microsoft BASIC is the ease with which you can program "special effects" on the screen, such as colour text and graphics. The particular features which you can use on your computer will depend on the sort of monitor you have. The examples in this chapter are written for an "elementary" monitor. This allows for text in 16 colours (40 or 80 characters per line), four colour medium resolution graphics (320 x 200 screen dots), and monochromatic high resolution graphics (640 x 200 screen dots).

Since this is a beginner's book, only the fundamentals are discussed here and in the summaries in the appendices. For the full treatment you will need to consult your particular computer manual.

The elementary monitor may be set in three distinct modes, using the SCREEN statement: text, medium resolution graphics and high resolution graphics. Each of these modes is discussed below.

12.1. Text Mode

This is the default mode. It may also be set with the statement

SCREEN 0

Hitting the special function key F10 has the same effect. The text display may be set to 40- or 80-column width with the statement

WIDTH n

where n is either 40 or 80.

The colour of each text character, and its background, may be set independently with the COLOR statement (BASIC originated in the United States of America: hence the spelling!). A character may also be made to blink on and off. For example, the statement

COLOR 17, 14, 5

anywhere in a program will cause any subsequent text characters to be in blinking blue on a yellow background, with a magenta border (the border is the area on the edge of the screen where no text appears). Try this out at once for the full technicolor effect! All these statements may also be entered directly as commands, in which case they have an immediate effect. The full range of colour codes is given in the summary in Appendix B.

12.2. Medium Resolution Colour Graphics

This mode is selected with the statement

SCREEN 1

In this mode, a dot (of chosen colour) may be put in any position on the screen, with horizontal co-ordinates from 0 to 319, and vertical co-ordinates from 0 to 199. The point (0; 0) is at the top left corner of the screen, and the point (319; 199) is at the bottom right corner. Text will be displayed over 40 columns.

Because of the dimensions of the screen, a square will not appear square on the screen. To make it appear so, the vertical co-ordinates should be multiplied by a scaling factor of 5/6. The CIRCLE statement, however (see below), does this scaling automatically, so that a circle drawn with this statement will appear round.

Once the screen mode has been selected with the SCREEN statement, the colour of the graphic images may be selected with the COLOR statement, the effect of which differs according to the screen mode. The COLOR statement in graphics mode has two arguments. The first selects the background colour, according to the values given in Appendix B under COLOR (Text). The second selects the "palette". There are two palettes, each with four colours: background, green, red and yellow; or background, cyan, magenta and white. The codes for selecting either palette, and the particular colour, are given in Appendix B under COLOR (Graphics).

12.2.1. Example: Traffic Lights

This example illustrates the basic concepts of medium resolution colour graphics. Two yellow circles of the same radius are drawn, one below the other. The area outside the circles is coloured yellow. The top circle is painted red, and then blacked out, after which the bottom one is painted green, and then blacked out. The process is repeated a few times. Details of the graphics statements are given in Appendix B.

```
100   REM RED AND GREEN TRAFFIC LIGHTS
110
120   KEY OFF                          'SWITCHES OFF KEY DISPLAY
130   CLS
140   SCREEN 1                         'SELECTS COLOUR GRAPHICS
150   COLOR 0, 0                       'SELECTS BACKGROUND AND PALETTE
160   CIRCLE( 160, 70 ), 30, 3         'DRAWS TOP CIRCLE
170   CIRCLE( 160, 150 ), 30, 3        'DRAWS BOTTOM CIRCLE
180   PAINT( 0, 0 ), 3                 'PAINTS AREA OUTSIDE YELLOW
190
200   FOR I = 1 TO 5
210      PAINT( 160, 70 ), 2, 3        'PAINTS TOP CIRCLE RED
220      FOR K = 1 TO 1000
230      NEXT K                        'PAUSES
240      PAINT( 160, 70 ), 0, 3        BLACKS IT OUT
250      PAINT( 160, 150 ), 1, 3       'PAINTS BOTTOM ONE GREEN
260      FOR K = 1 TO 2000
270      NEXT K                        'PAUSES FOR LONGER
280      PAINT( 160, 150 ), 0, 3       'BLACKS IT OUT
```

```
290  NEXT I
300  END
```

To get back into 80-column text mode after running such an example, hit the F10 key and then type the command WIDTH 80.

12.2.2. Example: Repayment of a Loan

If a loan is paid back in equal monthly instalments, where interest is compounded monthly, before the monthly repayment is made, the formula for repaying the loan with k equal repayments P is given by

$$P = [rA (1 + r)^k] / [(1 + r)^k - 1]$$

where A is the original amount of the loan, and r is the annual interest rate divided by 12. The outstanding loan balance B at the end of month n is then given by

$$B = A (1 + r)^n - P [(1 + r)^n - 1]/ r$$

The outstanding balance decreases very slowly at first, which is always rather depressing for new home owners, but the rate of decrease picks up rapidly toward the end of the repayment period, as the following program illustrates. A graph is drawn depicting the outstanding balance as time goes on for a loan of $50000 over 20 years (i.e. 240 months), at an annual interest rate of 20%.

```
100  REM BOND REPAYMENT
110
120  CLS
130  KEY OFF
140  SCREEN 1
150  COLOR 0, 0
160  SC = 0.002                            'VERTICAL SCALE FACTOR
170
180  READ R, AMT, K                        'RATE, AMOUNT, REPAYMENT PERIOD
190  R = R / 12                            'MONTHLY INTEREST RATE
200  P = R * AMT * (1 + R) ^ K / ( (1 + R) ^ K - 1)    'PAYMENT
210
220  PSET( 0, 100), 3
230  DRAW "C3R320"                         'HORIZONTAL (TIME) AXIS
240  GOSUB 420
250  PSET( 0, 100), 3
260  DRAW "C3U100"                         'VERTICAL (MONEY) AXIS
270  GOSUB 490
280  PSET( 0, 100 - SC * AMT), 3
290
300  FOR N = 1 TO K
310     BAL = AMT * (1 + R) ^ N - P * ( (1 + R) ^ N - 1 ) / R
320     LINE - ( N, 100 - SC * BAL ), 3    'DRAW THE CURVE
330  NEXT N
340
350  PAINT( 2, 98 ), 2, 3                  'PAINT IT RED!
360  LOCATE 15                             'MOVE CURSOR DOWN
370  PRINT "OUTSTANDING LOAN BALANCE AGAINST TIME"
380  LOCATE 24
390  DATA 0.2, 50000, 240
400  END
```

```
410
420    REM DRAW TIC MARKS ON HORIZONTAL AXIS
430      FOR IX = 20 TO 320 STEP 20
440        PSET( IX, 100 ), 3
450        DRAW "C3U2"
460      NEXT IX
470    RETURN
480
490    REM DRAW TIC MARKS ON VERTICAL AXIS
500      FOR IY = 80 TO 0 STEP −20
510        PSET( 0, IY ), 3
520        DRAW "C3R2"
530      NEXT IY
540    RETURN
```

Note that to get the graph the right way up with the horizontal axis at position 100, the vertical co-ordinate must be subtracted from 100 (after suitable scaling), as is done in lines 280 and 320.

The LINE statement (see Appendix B for details) is used to draw the actual graph. In this form, the statement

LINE − (X, Y)

will draw a line from the current pen position to the point (X; Y) in the specified colour (yellow in this case).

12.2.3. Example: Chook-Puff Animation

The next example shows how easily animation of graphic images may be achieved. A little cyan steam engine is made to run across the screen on a white railway line, puffing clouds of magenta smoke. The number of puffs of smoke in the smoke trail may be adjusted in the program.

In order to do this, a picture of the engine is drawn and then stored in the array CHOOK using the GET statement. Subsequent invocations of the PUT statement draw the same image at the specified place on the screen. However, when any points are drawn on top of points of the same colour, they cancel each other out, leaving a blank on the screen. In this way the image can be made to move across the screen.

```
100    REM CHOOK-PUFF ANIMATION
110
120    DIM CHOOK( 100 )                   'PICTURE OF ENGINE
130    DIM PUFF( 100 )                    'PICTURE OF SMOKE
140
150    CLS
160    KEY OFF
170    SCREEN 1
180    COLOR 0, 1                         'SELECT PALETTE 1
190    DX = 4                             'STEP-LENGTH FOR ANIMATION
200    NUMPUF = 5                         'NUMBER OF PUFFS IN SMOKE TRAIL
210
220    REM FIRST DRAW THE RAILWAY LINE ...
230    PSET( 0, 114 ), 3
240    DRAW "C3R320"
```

```
250
260   REM THEN THE ENGINE ...
270   PSET( 0, 100), 1
280   CHK1$ = "C1R5D5R8U5R2D5R1D6L1D2L2U2L6"
290   CHK2$ = "D2L2U2L2D2L2U2L1U6R3U3L3U2"
300   CHK$ = CHK1$ + CHK2$
310   DRAW CHK$
320   PAINT( 10, 108), 1
330   GET( 0, 100 ) – ( 16, 113 ), CHOOK
340
350   REM THEN THE PUFF OF SMOKE ...
360   PSET( 15, 94 ), 2
370   SMOKE$ = "C2U1R1U1R1U1L1U1L1U1L3D1L1D1L1D1R1D1R1D1R3"
380   DRAW SMOKE$
390   PAINT( 14, 93 ), 2
400   PRINT CHR$( 7 )                          'BLOW THE HOOTER!
410   GET( 10, 94 ) – ( 17, 89 ), PUFF
420
430   REM NOW SEND IT ALONG THE LINE LEAVING A TRAIL OF SMOKE ...
450   FOR IX = DX TO 300 STEP DX
460      PUT( IX – DX, 100 ), CHOOK           'RUB OUT THE OLD ENGINE
470      PUT( IX, 100 ), CHOOK                'DRAW THE NEW ONE
480      IF IX MOD 4 * DX = 0 THEN GOSUB 520
490   NEXT IX
500
510   END
520   REM PUFF THE SMOKE EVERY 4TH STEP
530      PUT( IX + 10, 89 ), PUFF
540      PRINT CHR$( 7 )
550      XPOS = IX + 10 – 4 * NUMPUF * DX     'BLOT OUT LAST PUFF
560      IF XPOS >= 0 THEN PUT( XPOS, 89 ), PUFF
570   RETURN
```

12.3. High Resolution Graphics

This mode is selected with the statement

SCREEN 2

The horizontal co-ordinates range from 0 to 639 (twice as many points as for medium resolution), and the vertical range from 0 to 199 (the same as for medium resolution). Text is displayed over 80 columns. The high resolution display is monochromatic on the "elementary" screen.

To make a square look square on the screen, the vertical co-ordinates must be multiplied by a scaling factor of 5/12.

12.3.1. Example: *Angle of Launch for Maximum Range*

This program is an example of interactive graphics. The problem is to find, by trial and error, the launch angle for a projectile to give it the maximum horizontal range (see §6.2 for the equations of motion). After each attempt, the trajectory of the projectile is left on the screen, together with the best angle used so far. The program is stopped by entering a negative launch angle. Note that nested WHILE-WEND statements are used.

SPECIAL TEXT AND GRAPHICS FACILITIES

```
100   REM TO FIND ANGLE OF LAUNCH FOR MAXIMUM RANGE
110
120   KEY OFF
130   CLS
140   SCREEN 2                            'SELECT HIGH RES MODE
150   PSET( 0, 0 )
160   DRAW "D199R639"                     'DRAW THE AXES
170   READ U, G, SC, DT                   'LAUNCH SPEED, ETC.
180   XMAX = 0                            'MAX RANGE
190   ANGMAX = 0                          'ANGLE FOR MAX RANGE
200   HD$ = "BEST SO FAR: ###.#"
210   LOCATE 1
220   PRINT USING HD$; ANGMAX
230   INPUT "ENTER LAUNCH ANGLE IN DEGREES (NEGATIVE TO STOP): ", ANG
240
250   WHILE ANG >= 0
260      AL = ANG * 3.141593 / 180        'CONVERT DEGREES TO RADIANS
270      Y = 0                            'HEIGHT DURING FLIGHT
280      PSET( 0, 199 )
290      T = 0                            'TIME IN FLIGHT
300
310      WHILE Y <= 199
320         T = T + DT
330         X = U * COS( AL ) * T
340         Y = 199 - SC * (U * SIN( AL ) * T - G * T ^ 2 / 2)
350         LINE - ( X, Y )
360      WEND
370
380      IF X > XMAX THEN GOSUB 480
390      LOCATE 1
400      PRINT "                                                              "
410      PRINT "                                                              "
420      LOCATE 1
430      PRINT USING HD$; ANGMAX
440      INPUT "ENTER LAUNCH ANGLE IN DEGREES (NEGATIVE TO STOP): ", ANG
450   WEND
460   END
470
480   REM REPLACE XMAX AND ANGMAX
490      XMAX = X
500      ANGMAX = ANG
510   RETURN
520   DATA 78, 9.8, 0.6, 0.25
```

12.4. Graphs on the Line Printer

Rough graphs can easily be produced on the printer using the TAB function. In the following program, one complete cycle of the graph of $sin(x)$ is printed.

```
100   REM GRAPH OF SIN(X)
120   Pi = 4 * ATN( 1 )                   ' CUNNING WAY TO GET Pi
140   PRINT "   X" TAB(37) "SIN(X)"
150   PRINT "   =" TAB(37) "===="
160   PRINT
165
170   FOR X = 0 TO 2 * Pi STEP Pi/20
180      PRINT USING "##.###"; X;
```

```
190    N = CINT( 25 * ( 1 + SIN( X ) ) )
200    N = 15 + N
210    IF N < 40 THEN PRINT TAB(N) " * " TAB(40) "."         ' SIN < 0
220    IF N > 40 THEN PRINT TAB(40) "." TAB(N) " * "         ' SIN > 0
230    IF N = 40 THEN PRINT TAB(N) " * "                     ' SIN = 0
240    NEXT X
250
260    END
```

The output is as follows.

X	SIN(X)
0.000	
0.157	
0.314	
0.471	
0.628	
0.785	
0.942	
1.100	
1.257	
1.414	
1.571	
1.728	
1.885	
2.042	
2.199	
2.356	
2.513	
2.670	
2.827	
2.985	
3.142	
3.299	
3.456	
3.613	
3.770	
3.927	
4.084	
4.241	
4.398	
4.555	
4.712	
4.869	
5.027	
5.184	
5.341	
5.498	
5.655	
5.812	
5.969	
6.126	
6.283	

More complicated graphs can be printed with the aid of the LOCATE statement (see Appendix B).

12.5. EXERCISES

12.1 The Spiral of Archimedes may be represented in polar co-ordinates by the equation

$r = at$

where r is the distance along a ray from the origin making an angle t with some axis (t is in radians), and a is some constant. (The shells of a class of animal called nummulites grow in this way.) Write a program to draw the spiral in high resolution for some values of a.

12.2 Another type of spiral is the logarithmic spiral, which describes the growth of shells of animals like the periwinkle and the nautilis. Its equation is

$r = aq^t$

where r and t are as above, and $a > 0, q > 1$. Write a program to draw this spiral.

12.3 The arrangement of seeds in a sunflower head (and other flowers, like daisies, for that matter) follows a fixed mathematical pattern. The nth seed is at position

$r = \sqrt{n}$

with angular co-ordinate $\pi dn/180$ radians, where d is the constant angle of divergence (in degrees) between any two successive seeds (i.e. between the nth and (n+1)th seeds). If $d = 137.51°$ one gets a perfect sunflower head. Write a program to plot the seeds in high resolution graphics. (Either use a point for each seed, or construct an image to represent each seed.) A remarkable feature of this is that the angle d must be exact to get proper sunflowers. Experiment with some different values, e.g.

137.45°: spokes fairly far out;
137.65°: spokes all the way (34 of them);
137.92°: Catherine wheels.

For further reading on this very interesting subject (Fibonacci numbers get into it somehow!) see the following:

Dixon R. The Mathematical Daisy, *New Scientist* (17 December 1981), pp. 792-5.

Ridley J.N. Packing Efficiency in Sunflower Heads, *Mathematical Biosciences*, Vol. 58 (1983) pp. 129-39.

13 MATRICES

Matrices are two-dimensional arrays which are used in a wide variety of representations. For example, the distances between nodes of a network, or a transportation scheme, or a co-ordinate transformation may all be represented as matrices (or tables). The computer needs to be told that it is dealing with matrices, as opposed to simple variables, or lists, and this is done through a DIM statement.

13.1. A Concrete Example

A concrete company has three concrete factories (S1, S2 and S3) which must supply three building sites (D1, D2 and D3). The costs of transporting a load of concrete from any factory to any site are given by the following table:

	D1	D2	D3
S1	3	12	10
S2	17	18	35
S3	7	10	24

The factories can supply 4, 12 and 8 loads per day respectively, and the sites require 10, 9 and 5 loads per day respectively. The real problem is to find the cheapest way to satisfy the demands at the sites, but we are not considering that here.

Suppose the factory manager proposes the following transportation scheme (each entry represents the number of loads of concrete to be transported on that particular route:

	D1	D2	D3
S1	4	—	—
S2	6	6	—
S3	—	3	5

This sort of scheme is called a solution to the transportation problem. The cost table (and the solution) can then be represented by matrices **C** and **X**, say, where c_{ij} is the entry in row i and column j of the cost table, e.g. $c_{23} = 35$.

To compute the cost of the above solution, each entry in the solution table must be multiplied by the corresponding entry in the cost table (this operation is not to be confused with matrix multiplication, which is dealt with in the next section). The following program will do what is required:

```
010    DIM C( 3,3 )              ' TABLE OF COSTS
015    DIM X( 3,3 )              ' SOLUTION
020    GOSUB 200
025    GOSUB 300
```

```
030  T = 0
040  FOR I = 1 TO 3
050    FOR J = 1 TO 3
060      T = T + C( I,J ) * X( I,J )
070    NEXT J
080  NEXT I
100  PRINT USING "TOTAL COST: $$###.##"; T
110  DATA 3, 12, 10, 17, 18, 35, 7, 10, 24
120  DATA 4, 0, 0, 6, 6, 0, 0, 3, 5
130  END
140
200  REM READ MATRIX C HERE
210  FOR I = 1 TO 3
220    FOR J = 1 TO 3
230      READ C( I,J )
240    NEXT J
250  NEXT I
260  RETURN
270
300  REM READ MATRIX X HERE
310  FOR I = 1 TO 3
320    FOR J = 1 TO 3
330      READ X( I,J )
340    NEXT J
350  NEXT I
360  RETURN
```

Note:

1) The maximum sizes of all matrices are declared in DIM statements at the beginning of the program.

2) After the READs have been executed, the arrays in memory will look as follows:

	C		X	
C(1,1)	3	X(1,1)	4
C(1,2)	12	X(1,2)	0
C(1,3)	10	X(1,3)	0
C(2,1)	17	X(2,1)	6
C(2,2)	18	X(2,2)	6
C(2,3)	35	X(2,3)	0
C(3,1)	7	X(3,1)	0
C(3,2)	10	X(3,2)	3
C(3,3)	24	X(3,3)	5

Thus the first subscript refers to the matrix "row", and the second to its "column". This is the standard convention.

3) The coding for handling matrices can get rather long, and tends to slow down a program. A colon (:) may be used in such cases to get more than one statement on a line, thus speeding up execution time. Counters should also be of integer type. Lines 210-250 can then be rewritten as:

```
210  FOR I% = 1 TO 3: FOR J% = 1 TO 3
220    READ C( I%,J% )
230  NEXT J%: NEXT I%
```

In general a matrix is usually denoted by a capital letter, e.g. **A**, and each entry or element of the matrix is denoted by the small letter of the same name followed by two subscripts, the first indicating the row of the element, and the second indicating the column. So a general element of the matrix **A** is called a_{ij}, meaning it may be found in row i and column j. If **A** has three rows and three columns (3x3 for short) it will look like this in general:

$$\begin{bmatrix} a_{11} & a_{12} & a_{13} \\ a_{21} & a_{22} & a_{23} \\ a_{31} & a_{32} & a_{33} \end{bmatrix}.$$

If, for example,

$$\mathbf{A} = \begin{bmatrix} 6 & 2 & 0 \\ -1 & 4 & 7 \\ 5 & 1 & 13 \end{bmatrix},$$

then $a_{21} = -1$; $a_{23} = 7$; $a_{31} = 5$; and so on.

13.2. Matrix Multiplication

Various mathematical operations are defined on matrices. Multiplication is probably the most important such operation, and is used widely in such areas as network theory, solution of linear systems of equations, transformation of co-ordinate systems, and population modelling.

When two matrices, **A** and **B**, are multiplied together, their product is a third matrix, which we may as well call **C**. The operation is written as

C = AB ,

and the general element c_{ij} of **C** is formed by taking the scalar product of the ith row of **A** with the jth column of **B**. It follows then that **A** and **B** can only be successfully multiplied (in that order) if the number of columns in **A** is the same as the number of rows in **B**.

Definition:

If **A** is a *nxm* matrix, and **B** is a *mxp* matrix, their product **C** will be a *nxp* matrix defined so that the general element c_{ij} *of* **C** is given by

$$c_{ij} = \sum_{k=1}^{m} a_{ik} b_{kj}$$

Note that in general **AB** is NOT equal to **BA** (matrix multiplication is not commutative).

Examples:

$$\begin{bmatrix} 1 & 2 \\ 3 & 4 \end{bmatrix} \times \begin{bmatrix} 5 & 6 \\ 0 & -1 \end{bmatrix} = \begin{bmatrix} 5 & 4 \\ 15 & 14 \end{bmatrix} ;$$

$$\begin{bmatrix} 1 & 2 \\ 3 & 4 \end{bmatrix} \times \begin{bmatrix} 2 \\ 3 \end{bmatrix} = \begin{bmatrix} 8 \\ 18 \end{bmatrix} .$$

The following program uses the subroutine in lines 1000–1140 to multiply two matrices **A** and **B**, and store their product in **C**. The dimensions of the matrices must be specified before the subroutine is evoked. The program is run with the first two matrices given above as data.

```
100   REM TEST PROGRAM FOR MATRIX MULTIPLICATION
110   DIM A(2,2)
120   DIM B(2,2)
130   DIM C(2,2)
140   READ M, N, P                    ' ALL MATRICES SQUARE IN THIS EXAMPLE
145
150   FOR I = 1 TO N: FOR J = 1 TO N
160     READ A(I,J)
170   NEXT J: NEXT I
180
210   FOR I = 1 TO N: FOR J = 1 TO N
220     READ B(I,J)
230   NEXT J: NEXT I
240
270   GOSUB 1000                      'MULTIPLY THEM
280
290   FOR I = 1 TO N: FOR J = 1 TO N
300     PRINT USING "###"; C(I,J);
310   NEXT J: PRINT: NEXT I
325
330   DATA 2, 2, 2
340   DATA 1, 2, 3, 4
350   DATA 5, 6, 0, -1
360   END
370
1000  REM MATRIX MULTIPLICATION:
1010  REM Multiplies A (NxM) by B (MxP) and stores product in
1020  REM .. C (NxP).
1030  REM ALL MATRICES MUST BE SUITABLY DIMENSIONED IN MAIN PROG
1040
1050  FOR I = 1 TO N
1060    FOR J = 1 TO P
1070      C(I,J) = 0                  'BLOT IT OUT JUST IN CASE!
1080      FOR K = 1 TO M
1090        C(I,J) = C(I,J) + A(I,K) * B(K,J)
1100      NEXT K
1110    NEXT J
1120  NEXT I
1130
1140  RETURN
```

RUN
5 4
15 14

N.B. Great care must be taken that the subscripts I, J and K used in the subroutine do not get muddled up with counters in other FOR-NEXT loops elsewhere in the program!

Since the routine in lines 1000-1140 can be used in any program that needs matrix multiplication, it may be convenient to save it separately and to "merge" it into any program that needs it. The following variation on the command SAVE must be used (delete lines 100-370 first):

SAVE "MATRIX", A

The A option ensures that the coding is saved in ASCII format rather than compressed binary. Whenever the routine is needed in the workspace, the command

MERGE "MATRIX"

will add the subroutine to the program currently in the workspace (as opposed to LOAD which erases the current program). For MERGE to work it is essential that the required coding be saved with the A option before merging.

13.3. Transformation of a Co-ordinate System

If you have done some university mathematics you may recall that when a Cartesian co-ordinate system is rotated counterclockwise through an angle a the new co-ordinates $(x'; y')$ of a point in the rotated system are given by

$x' = x \cos(a) + y \sin(a)$
$y' = -x \sin(a) + y \cos(a)$

where $(x; y)$ are its co-ordinates before rotation. This transformation may be written more concisely using matrix multiplication:

X' = **A X**

where $\mathbf{A} = \begin{bmatrix} \cos(a) & \sin(a) \\ -\sin(a) & \cos(a) \end{bmatrix}$

and $\mathbf{X} = \begin{bmatrix} x \\ y \end{bmatrix}$, $\mathbf{X}' = \begin{bmatrix} x' \\ y' \end{bmatrix}$

The next program reads an angle of rotation (given in degrees), the x− and y− co-ordinates of a point in the unrotated system, and computes its co-ordinates after rotation (the unit point on the x-axis is used as sample data in a rotation of 30°):

```
100  REM CO-ORDINATE TRANSFORMATION
110  DIM A( 2,2 )              'TRANSFORMATION MATRIX
120  DIM B( 2,1 )              'OLD CO-ORDS
130  DIM C( 2,1 )              'NEW CO-ORDS
```

```
140
150   READ ANG, B( 1,1 ), B( 2,1 )
160   ANG = ANG * 3.141593 / 180        'CONVERT TO RADIANS
170   M = 2: N = 2: P = 1               'DIMENSIONS OF MATRIX & VECTORS
190
200   REM SET UP TRANSFORMATION MATRIX
210   A( 1,1 ) = COS( ANG )
220   A( 1,2 ) = SIN( ANG )
230   A( 2,1 ) = - A( 1,2 )
240   A( 2,2 ) = A( 1,1 )
250
260   GOSUB 1000                        'REMEMBER TO MERGE!
270
280   PRINT "OLD CO-ORDINATES: ";
290   PRINT USING "###.####"; B( 1,1 ), B( 2,1 )
310   PRINT "NEW CO-ORDINATES: ";
320   PRINT USING "###.####"; C( 1,1 ), C( 2,1 )
320   DATA 30, 1, 0
330   END
MERGE "MATRIX"
RUN
OLD CO-ORDINATES:      1.0000    0.0000
NEW CO-ORDINATES:      0.8660  -0.5000
```

The curious DIM statements in lines 120 and 130 are needed to trick the program into thinking that B and C are matrices (necessary if the routine in lines 1000- is to be used unchanged) when in fact they are really vectors with two rows and one column each.

Once the transformation matrix in lines 210-240 has been set up the program could be adapted to rotate a figure on a graphics screen (if you have one) by applying the transformation to each point in the figure in turn.

13.4. Reachability Matrix of a Network

Suppose five spies in an espionage ring have the code names Alex, Boris, Cyril, Denisov, and Eric (whom we can number for the sake of argument with the subtle numerical codes of 1, 2, 3, 4, and 5 respectively). The hallmark of a good spy network is that each agent is not able to contact all the others. The arrangement for this particular group is: Alex can contact only Cyril (and NOT vice-versa); Boris can contact only Alex or Eric; Denisov can contact only Cyril; Eric can contact only Cyril or Denisov.

The need for good spies to be versed in matrix theory becomes apparent when one spots that the possible paths of communication can be represented by a 5x5 matrix, with rows representing transmitting agents, and columns representing receiving agents, thus:

	A	B	C	D	E
A	0	0	1	0	0
B	1	0	0	0	1
C	0	0	0	0	0
D	0	0	1	0	0
E	0	0	1	1	0

We will call this matrix **A**. It clearly represents a directed network with the spies at the nodes, and with arcs all of length one. It may also be thought of as an "adjacency" matrix, with a one in row i and column j if there is an arc from node i to node j, or a zero in that position if there is no arc between those two nodes. The diagonal elements of **A** (i.e. a_{11}, a_{22}, etc.) are all zero, because good spies do not talk to themselves (since they might then talk in their sleep and give themselves away).

Now from this adjacency matrix we can see, for example, that Boris can contact Eric, who in turn can contact Cyril. We can say therefore then there is a "path" through the network from Boris to Cyril, or that Cyril is "reachable" from Boris. We would in general like to know who is reachable from whom, and in how many different ways.

There is a algorithm to determine which nodes in a network may be reached from any node (reachability). We will use the algorithm without proving that it works, or why it works, although that is not difficult (see Hahn 1987, for a detailed discussion of reachability). For our 5 node network, the algorithm requires that we compute a "reachability" matrix **R** as follows:

$$R = A + A^2 + A^3 + A^4.$$

R will also be a 5x5 matrix, and its elements give the total number of paths of communication between the agents. The following program computes the reachability matrix for our spy ring:

```
100   REM REACHABILITY
110   DIM A( 5,5 )                'ADJACENCY MATRIX
120   DIM B( 5,5 )                'WORKING SPACE
130   DIM C( 5,5 )                'WORKING SPACE
150   DIM R( 5,5 )                'REACHABILITY MATRIX
160                               '
170   READ M, N, P                'DIMENSIONS OF MATRICES
180   FOR I = 1 TO N: FOR J = 1 TO N
190      READ A( I,J )
200   NEXT J: NEXT I
210                               '
240   GOSUB 2000                  'COPY A INTO R AND B
250                               '
270   FOR L = 1 TO N−2
280      GOSUB 1000               'C = A x B
290      GOSUB 4000               'B = C
300      GOSUB 5000               'R = R + B
310   NEXT L
320                               '
330   FOR I = 1 TO N: FOR J = 1 TO N
340      PRINT USING "###"; R( I,J );
350   NEXT J: PRINT: NEXT I
390                               '
400   DATA 5, 5, 5
410   DATA 0, 0, 1, 0, 0
420   DATA 1, 0, 0, 0, 1
430   DATA 0, 0, 0, 0, 0
440   DATA 0, 0, 1, 0, 0
450   DATA 0, 0, 1, 1, 0
460   END
```

```
470
2000   REM COPY A INTO R AND B
2010   FOR I = 1 TO N: FOR J = 1 TO N
2020     R( I,J ) = A( I,J )
2030     B( I,J ) = A( I,J )
2040   NEXT J: NEXT I
2050   RETURN
2060
4000   REM COPY C INTO B
4010   FOR I = 1 TO N: FOR J = 1 TO N
4020     B( I,J ) = C( I,J )
4030   NEXT J: NEXT I
4040   RETURN
4050
5000   REM REPLACE R BY R + B
5010   FOR I = 1 TO N: FOR J = 1 TO N
5020     R( I,J ) = R( I,J ) + B( I,J )
5030   NEXT J: NEXT I
5040   RETURN
MERGE "MATRIX"
RUN
0  0  1  0  0
1  0  3  1  1
0  0  0  0  0
0  0  1  0  0
0  0  2  1  0
```

The program as it stands takes about 11 seconds to run on an IBM PC, because of all the matrix manipulation. Declaring all variables integer (with DEFINT A-Z at the beginning) reduces the execution time to about 8 seconds.

If you can't follow the program, work through it by hand, keeping track of the matrices. E.g. the effect of line 240 is to make

R = A and
B = A.

Going through the FOR-NEXT loop in lines 270-310 the first time has the effect:

C = A x B (= A x A, since B = A)
B = C (= A x A)
R = R + B (= A + A x A)

If you go on like this for N-2 repeats of the loop you will see that R has the final form as given above.

So we can read off from the reachability matrix R the fact that there are, for example, three different paths of communication between Boris and Cyril, but only two between Eric and Cyril. The name "reachability" is used because the non-zero elements of **R** indicate which agents may contact which, directly or indirectly, or for a distance network, which nodes may be reached from each node.

In general, the reachability matrix **R** of a network with N nodes may be defined as the sum of the first $(N-1)$ powers of the adjacency matrix **A** associated with the network, i.e.

$$R = A + A^2 + A^3 + ... + A^{N-1}.$$

13.5. Calculation of Volumes of Excavation

A problem that arises in the building industry is the calculation of the volume of earth to be excavated on a site. We assume that the excavation is to have a rectangular level base and vertical sides. The area to be excavated is surveyed, and the heights of the ground above the excavation base are found, on a 10 metre square grid, let us say. So a section of a plan of such an excavation could look something like this:

```
              A              B              C
   3      3 | 95 _____  3 | 86 _____  3 | 56

   2      2 | 95 _____  2 | 85 _____  2 | 48

   1      2 | 45 _____  3 | 10 _____  3 | 00
```

The numbers are the heights above the excavation base in centimetres. Consider the square bounded by A3, B3, A2 and B2. The volume of the vertical square prism excavated beneath it is the horizontal plan area times the average height of the corners above the base, i.e.

Volume = 10 x 10 x (3.95 + 3.86 + 2.85 + 2.95) / 4 cubic metres.

We could do this for every vertical square prism to be excavated and add up all the volumes so calculated. However, an easier way presents itself if we notice that some corner heights are used in four squares, some in two squares, and some in only one, as shown below:

Grid pt	Corner ht	No. of squares (n) corner appears in	n x corner ht
A3	3.95	1	3.95
B3	3.86	2	7.72
C3	3.56	1	3.56
A2	2.95	2	5.90
B2	2.85	4	11.40
C2	2.48	2	4.96
A1	2.45	1	2.45
B1	3.10	2	6.20
C1	3.00	1	3.00
		TOTAL:	49.14

From this table, the volume to be excavated may then be calculated as

   10 x 10 x 49.14 / 4   = 1228.5   cubic metres.

In general, the corner heights may obviously be represented by a matrix **H**, say, where a particular height is given by $H(i,j)$, and where i and j label the rows and columns of the grid respectively. Let us suppose there are m rows and n columns in the grid. The contributions of the heights to the total volume are as follows:

Corners in 1 square: $H(1,1) + H(1,n) + H(m,1) + H(m,n)$

Corners in 2 squares: $\displaystyle 2 \sum_{i=2}^{m-1} [H(i, 1) + H(i, n)] + 2 \sum_{j=2}^{n-1} [H(1, j) + H(m, j)]$

Corners in 4 squares: $\displaystyle 4 \sum_{i=2}^{m-1} \sum_{j=2}^{n-1} H(i, j)$

This sort of calculation is
what computers were invented for. As an example, the program below computes the volume of excavation under a 5x10 grid (i.e. $m = 5$ and $n = 10$: 50 grid points altogether).

```
100   REM VOLUME OF EXCAVATION
110   DIM H( 5,10 )                                   '5x10 GRID
120                                                   '
130   M = 5                                           '5 ROWS
140   N = 10                                          '10 COLUMNS
142                                                   '
144   FOR I = 1 TO M: FOR J = 1 TO N
146      READ H( I,J )
148   NEXT J: NEXT I
149                                                   '
150   V1 = 0                                          'CORNERS IN 1 SQ
160   V2 = 0                                          'CORNERS IN 2 SQS
170   V4 = 0                                          'CORNERS IN 4 SQS
180                                                   '
190   V1 = H( 1,1 ) + H( 1,N ) + H( M,1 ) + H( M,N )
200                                                   '
210   FOR I = 2 TO M−1
220      V2 = V2 + 2 * ( H( I,1 ) + H( I,N ) )
230   NEXT I
240                                                   '
250   FOR J = 2 TO N−1
260      V2 = V2 + 2 * ( H( 1,J ) + H( M,J ) )
270   NEXT J
280                                                   '
290   FOR I = 2 TO M−1
300      FOR J = 2 TO N−1
310         V4 = V4 + 4 * H( I,J )
320      NEXT J
330   NEXT I
340                                                   '
350   V = 100 * ( V1 + V2 + V4 ) / 4                  'TOTAL VOLUME
355                                                   '
360   PRINT USING "VOLUME EXCAVATED: ######.## CUBIC METRES"; V
380   DATA 3.95, 3.86, 3.56 ....
390   DATA 2.95, 2.85, 2.48 ....
400   DATA 2.45, 3.10, 3.00 ....
410   DATA ....
420   DATA ....
430   END
```

To handle grids of different sizes, the only changes that need to be made are in lines 110, 130 and 140, and in the DATA statements.

13.6. Area of a Site

A problem which arises in land surveying is the calculation of the area of a plot of ground. Assuming the sides of the plot to be straight, this amounts to finding the area of a irregular polygon, i.e. an n-sided figure with straight sides. Although the computation that is described below doesn't actually use matrices directly, the algorithm used exploits a mathematical property of matrices: the determinant. Considering the 3x3 matrix

$$A = \begin{bmatrix} a_{11} & a_{12} & a_{13} \\ a_{21} & a_{22} & a_{23} \\ a_{31} & a_{32} & a_{33} \end{bmatrix}$$

its determinant D is defined as

$$\begin{aligned} D = & a_{11}(a_{22}a_{33} - a_{23}a_{32}) \\ & + a_{12}(a_{23}a_{31} - a_{21}a_{33}) \\ & + a_{13}(a_{21}a_{32} - a_{22}a_{31}) \end{aligned}$$

Now consider the triangle in the figure below.

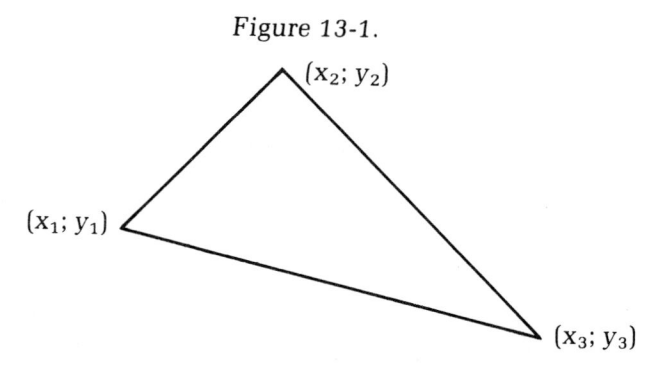

Figure 13-1.

If the positions of its vertices are represented by Cartesian co-ordinates in the usual way, the area of the triangle may be given as

$$\text{Area} = 0.5 \times \text{Det} \begin{bmatrix} 1 & 1 & 1 \\ y_1 & y_2 & y_3 \\ x_1 & x_2 & x_3 \end{bmatrix}$$

where *Det* stands for determinant (this is not too difficult to prove: drop perpendiculars from the vertices to the x-axis and use the areas of the resulting trapezia in the figure to find the area of the triangle).

The point about this is that a polygon with N vertices may be broken up into $N-2$ triangles sharing a common vertex by drawing lines from the common vertex to each other vertex in turn, as shown in Fig. 13-2.

Figure 13-2.

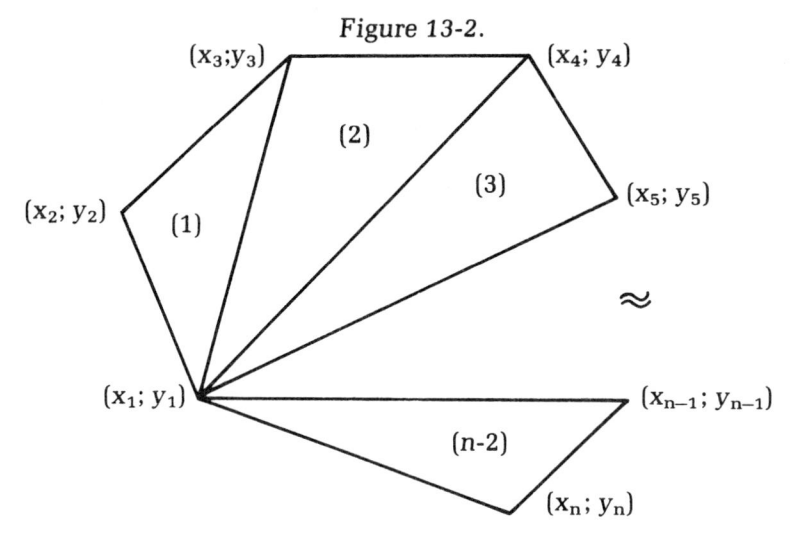

The area of the ith triangle (numbered from the left) in the composite figure is thus

$$0.5 \times \text{Det} \begin{bmatrix} 1 & 1 & 1 \\ y_1 & y_{i+1} & y_{i+2} \\ x_1 & x_{i+1} & x_{i+2} \end{bmatrix} \qquad (*)$$

as can easily be seen by writing out the expression for the areas of a 6-sided polygon, for example. The area of the N-sided polygon thus formed is the sum of the areas (*) for i running from 1 to N-2. The formula works, by the way, even if some of the interior angles of the polygon are reflex (> 180°). This is because the sign of a determinant changes if two rows or columns are interchanged (puzzle that one out if you like!).

The program that follows computes the area of a polygon, where the only restriction on the data is that the co-ordinates of the vertices must be given in order as one moves round the figure in a clockwise sense. The sample data in the program is for a 7-sided figure with one reflex angle (you can verify the result by drawing the figure on squared paper).

```
100  REM AREA OF A POLYGON
110  DIM X(20)                        'X CO-ORDS OF EACH CORNER
120  DIM Y(20)                        'Y CO-ORDS OF EACH CORNER
130  READ N
140  FOR I = 1 TO N
150     READ X(I), Y(I)               'CO-ORDS MUST BE GIVEN IN ORDER
160  NEXT I
170                                   ,
180  AREA = 0                         'AREA OF THE POLYGON
190  A11 = 1: A12 = 1
200  A13 = 1                          'CONSTANT TERMS IN THE DETERMINANT
205  A21 = X(1): A31 = Y(1)
210                                   ,
220  FOR I = 1 TO N-2
230     A22 = Y( I+1 )
240     A32 = X( I+1 )
```

```
250     A23 = Y( I+2 )
260     A33 = X( I+2 )
270     GOSUB 500                    'FOR THE DETERMINANT
280     AREA = AREA + DET / 2
290   NEXT I
300                                  ,
310   PRINT USING "AREA: ###.#"; AREA
320   END
330                                  ,
340   DATA 7
350   DATA  0,0,  -1,1,  0,2,  1,2,  1,1,  2,1,
2,0
360                                  ,
500   REM DETERMINANT OF A 3x3 MATRIX
510   D1 = A11 * (A22 * A33 - A23 * A32)
520   D2 = A12 * (A23 * A31 - A21 * A33)
530   D3 = A13 * (A21 * A32 - A22 * A31)
540   DET = D1 + D2 + D3
550   RETURN
RUN
AREA:   4.0
```

13.7. Special MAT Statements

Some versions of BASIC (not Microsoft BASIC unfortunately) have special statements that handle matrices as single entities, so that one doesn't have to bother about handling the subscripts at all. These statements are all preceded by the keyword MAT. For example, the single statement

n   MAT READ A

will read the matrix **A** (assuming that it has been correctly dimensioned in a DIM statement). With this facility, the reachability matrix program of §13.4 may be written in a far more readable form, as follows (note that the matrix multiplication subroutine is no longer required!):

```
100   DIM A( 5,5 )
110   DIM B( 5,5 )
120   DIM C( 5,5 )
135   DIM R( 5,5 )
140                                  ,
150   N = 5                          ' NO. OF NODES
160   MAT READ A                     ' ADJACENCY MATRIX
170   MAT R = A
180   MAT B = A
190                                  ,
200   FOR I = 1 TO N-2
210     MAT C = A * B
220     MAT B = C
230     MAT R = R + B                ' REACHABILITY
240   NEXT I
250                                  ,
260   MAT PRINT R;
270                                  ,
280   DATA 0, 0, 1, 0, 0
```

```
290  DATA 1, 0, 0, 0, 1
300  DATA 0, 0, 0, 0, 0
310  DATA 0, 0, 1, 0, 0
320  DATA 0, 0, 1, 1, 0
330
340  END
```

Another useful MAT function is INV, which inverts a matrix. It can be used in a program to solve simultaneous equations.

Consider the system of simultaneous equations:

$$2x - 4y + 3z = -9$$
$$3x - z = 4$$
$$2x + 5y + z = 11.$$

The system may be represented by matrices **A**, **B** and **X** if we define

$$A = \begin{bmatrix} 2 & -4 & 3 \\ 3 & 0 & -1 \\ 2 & 5 & 1 \end{bmatrix}$$

and

$$X = \begin{bmatrix} x \\ y \\ z \end{bmatrix} \qquad B = \begin{bmatrix} -9 \\ 4 \\ 11 \end{bmatrix}.$$

We can then write, in matrix form,

$$AX = B.$$

It can be shown mathematically that the solution vector **X** may be obtained as follows:

$$X = A^{-1}B,$$

where A^{-1} is the matrix inverse of **A**. It is usually a fairly complicated problem to write a program to use this scheme to solve a set of simultaneous equations, but with MAT statements it is almost trivial, as we see:

```
100  DIM A( 3,3 )
102  DIM C( 3,3 )
110  DIM B( 3,1 )
112  DIM X( 3,1 )
120  MAT READ A
130  MAT READ B
140  MAT C = INV( A )
150  MAT X = C * B
160  MAT PRINT X
170  DATA 2, -4, 3, 3, 0, -1, 2, 5, 1
180  DATA -9, 4, 11
190  END
```

The resulting output is:
    1
    2
   -1

i.e. the solution to the system is $x = 1$; $y = 2$; $z = -1$.

REFERENCE

Hahn B.D. *Problem Solving with FORTRAN 77*, Edward Arnold, London, 1987.

14 INTRODUCTION TO NUMERICAL METHODS

One of the major scientific uses of modern digital computers is in finding numerical solutions to mathematical problems which have no analytical solutions, i.e. solutions which may be written down in terms of polynomials and the known mathematical functions such as logarithms, sines, exponentials, etc. In this chapter we look briefly at three areas where numerical methods have been highly developed: solving equations, evaluating integrals and derivatives, and solving differential equations.

14.1. Equations

In this section we consider how to solve equations in one unknown numerically. The general way of expressing the problem is to say that we want to solve the equation

$$f(x) = 0 ,$$

i.e. we want to find the value(s) of x that make the LHS vanish, where $f(x)$ is any given function of x. Such a value of x is called a root of the equation. There are mathematical solutions for a very small class of functions f. For example, if $f(x)$ is a polynomial of order two (i.e. a quadratic equation), there is a well known formula for the solution. But there is no general method for finding an analytical solution for any given $f(x)$.

14.1.1. Newton's Method

This is perhaps the easiest numerical method for solving equations. The basic idea is as follows: given some initial guess at the root x, the method makes use of the derivative $f'(x)$ to improve the guess by computing $x\dagger$, say, which in general is closer to the root than the first guess. The process is continued until a required accuracy is achieved. Figure 14-1 illustrates Newton's method geometrically.

From the figure we see that

$$f'(x) = [f(x) - 0]/(x - x\dagger) .$$

Solving for $x\dagger$ gives

$$x\dagger = x - f(x)/f'(x) \tag{1}$$

Equ.(1) is Newton's algorithm. It is implemented as follows:

1. Read in a starting x, and required accuracy (acc)
2. Compute $x\dagger$ with Newton's method and replace x by $x\dagger$
3. Print x and $f(x)$
4. While $abs(f(x)) \geq acc$ repeat up to 20 times, say:

4.1 Compute x† with Newton's method and replace x by x†
4.2 Print x and f(x)
5. Stop.

Figure 14-1. Graphical derivation of Newton's method

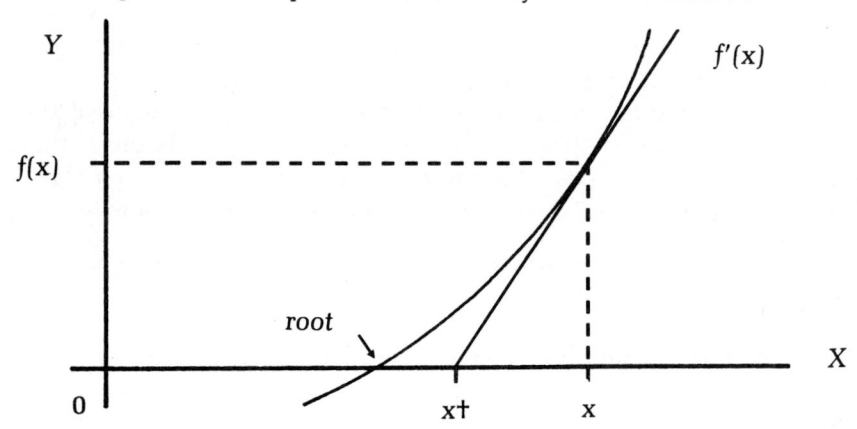

Example: Solve $x^3 + x - 3 = 0$.

The program to solve this problem is discussed in §11.2, where output for the initial guess x = 2 is given. It is often possible to make a reasonable initial guess by inspection.

The method is so simple that it can even be implemented on a calculator without much effort. The structure plan makes it clear that (1) Newton's algorithm is used at least once, and (2) there are two conditions which lead to the termination of the main loop.

Exercises:

1. Try running the program with different starting values of x to see whether the algorithm always converges.

2. Try to find a non-zero root of

   $2x = \tan x$

   using Newton's method.

You might experience some trouble with the second one. For example, the following output results if we start the algorithm with x = 2:

X	F(X)
3.639	−.6735E+01
5.905	0.1221E+02
8.585	−.1829E+02
84.325	−.1692E+03
.	

DIVERGED

The estimates of the root are clearly diverging. In fact the method has jumped past roots near 4.604, 7.79, etc., as can be seen by sketching the graph carefully. This highlights the only serious problem that arises with Newton's method: the algorithm only converges to a root if the starting guess is "close enough" to the root. And since "close enough" depends on $f(x)$ and on the root, one can obviously get into difficulties here. The only remedy is some intelligent trial and error work on the initial guess.

Newton's method may also fail if $f(x)$ is very "flat" near a root, since the algorithm requires division by $f'(x)$, which can get very small in this case. This can easily result in a floating point overflow. If the method fails to find a root, the Bisection method, as described in the next section, may be used.

Application

Newton's method may be built (hardwired) into calculators to evaluate reciprocals and nth roots, for example. To find the reciprocal of a number a amounts to solving the equation

$$f(x) = 1/x - a = 0 .$$

Applying equ.(1) to this form of $f(x)$ gives, after a little algebra,

$$x\dagger = x(2 - ax) .$$

Note that this requires no divisions: it was used on old fashioned computers with no division facility.

14.1.2. Example: Hire Purchase Rip-off

When an item is bought on so-called "hire purchase", the interest is calculated in advance in one lump sum, which is added to the capital amount, and then equally divided over the repayment period. For example, suppose the cash value of the item is $10 000, and equal monthly payments must be made over a period of three years. If the hire purchase interest rate is 25%, the payments are calculated by adding three times 25% of $10 000 to $10 000, and dividing the resultant sum by 36, giving repayments of $486 per month. The effect of this is that your total interest charges over the three-year period amount to $7 500 . It is extremely interesting, and revealing, to work out what effective nominal annual interest rate, compounded monthly on the reducing balance, would result in the same monthly repayments.

The problem amounts to solving the formula quoted in Ex. 2.18 for the unknown effective interest rate r, viz.

$$P = [(r/n) A(1 + r/n)^{nk}] / [(1 + r/n)^{nk} - 1] ,$$

where A is the cash value of the item, k the repayment period in years, n the number of repayment periods per year, and P the regular repayments. It is convenient to change the unknown to x , where

$x = 1 + r/n$.

If we re-arrange the expression for P , and define $f(x)$ as

$f(x) = Ax^{nk+1} - (A + P)x^{nk} + P$,

then we have to solve the equation

$f(x) = 0$,

which must be done with Newton's method. This requires the first derivative of $f(x)$, viz.

$f'(x) = (nk + 1)Ax^{nk} - nk(A + P)x^{nk-1}$.

The following program implements the numerical solution.

```
100   REM SOLVING FOR EFFECTIVE HIRE PURCHASE INTEREST RATE
120   REM VARIABLES HAVE SAME MEANINGS AS IN TEXT ABOVE
130
180   DEF FNF( X ) = A * X ^ (N.* K + 1) − (A + P) * X ^ (N * K) + P
190   DEF FNDF( X ) = (N * K + 1) * A * X ^ (N *K) − N * K * (A + P) * X ^ (N * K − 1)
200
210   CLS
220   INPUT "CASH VALUE: ", A
230   INPUT "REGULAR REPAYMENT: ", P
240   INPUT "REPAYMENT PERIOD IN YEARS: ", K
250   INPUT "NUMBER OF REPAYMENTS PER YEAR: ", N
260
280   X = 1.1
290   ITS = 0
300   MAX = 20
310   EPS = 1E−4
320
330   WHILE ABS( FNF( X ) ) >= EPS AND ITS < MAX
340      X = X − FNF( X ) / FNDF( X )
350      ITS = ITS + 1
370   WEND
380
390   IF ABS( FNF( X ) ) < EPS THEN GOSUB 420 ELSE PRINT "DIVERGED"
400   END
410
420   REM NEWTON CONVERGED
430      R = N * (X − 1)
440      PRINT
```

```
450    PRINT USING "RIP-OFF INTEREST RATE IS ###.#% _!"; 100 * R
460    RETURN
RUN
CASH VALUE: 10000
REGULAR REPAYMENT: 486
REPAYMENT PERIOD IN YEARS: 3
NUMBER OF REPAYMENTS PER YEAR: 12

RIP-OFF INTEREST RATE IS 40.8% !
```

14.1.3. The Bisection Method

Consider again the problem of solving the equation

$$f(x) = x^3 + x - 3 = 0.$$

We attempt to find by inspection, or trial and error, two values of x, call them xL and xR, such that $f(xL)$ and $f(xR)$ have different signs, i.e. $f(xL).f(xR) < 0$. If we can find two such values, the implication is that the root lies somewhere in the interval between xL and xR, since $f(x)$ changes sign on this interval (see Figure 14-2). In this example, xL = 1 and xR = 2 will do, since $f(1) = -1$ and $f(2) = 7$. In the Bisection method, we estimate the root by xM, where xM is the midpoint (hence the name "bisection") of the interval [xL; xR], i.e.

$$xM = (xL + xR)/2. \tag{2}$$

Then if $f(xM)$ has the same sign as $f(xL)$, as drawn in the figure, the root clearly lies between xM and xR. We must then redefine the left-hand end of the interval as having the value of xM, i.e. we let the new value of xL be xM. Otherwise, if $f(xM)$ and $f(xL)$ have different signs, we let the new value of xR be xM, since the root must lie between xL and xM in this case. Having redefined xL or xR as the case may be, we bisect again according to equ.(2) and

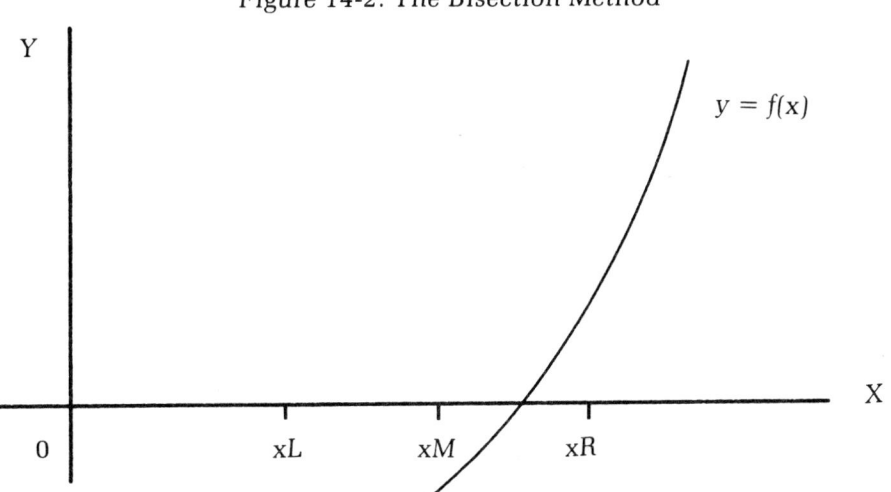

Figure 14-2. The Bisection Method

repeat the process until the distance between xL and xR is as small as we please.

The neat thing about this method is that we can calculate before starting how many bisections are needed to obtain a certain accuracy, given initial values of xL and xR. (With Newton's method, we can never be sure exactly how many iterations will be required.) Suppose we start with xL = a, and xR = b. After the first bisection the worst possible error, E_1, in xM is

$$E_1 = |a - b|/2 ,$$

since we are estimating the root as being at the midpoint of the interval [a; b]. The worst that can happen is that the root is actually at xL or xR, in which case the error is E_1. After the second bisection, the error E_2 will obviously be half of E_1, i.e.

$$E_2 = |a - b|/4 = |a - b|/2^2 .$$

Carrying on like this, after n bisections the worst possible error E_n is given by

$$E_n = |a - b|/2^n.$$

If we want to be sure that this is less than some specified error E, we must see to it that n satisfies the inequality

$$|a - b|/2^n < E,$$

i.e. $\quad 2^n > |a - b|/E ,$

i.e. $\quad n \log(2) > \log[\,|a - b|/E] ,$

i.e. $\quad n > \log[|a - b|/E]/\log(2) \hfill (3)$

Since n is the number of bisections, it must be an integer. The smallest integer n that exceeds the RHS of inequality (3) will do as the maximum number of bisections required to guarantee the given accuracy E.

The following scheme may be used to program the Bisection method. It will work for any function f(x) that changes sign (in either direction) between the two values xL and xR, which must be found beforehand by the user.

1. Read a,b and E
2. Initialise xL and xR
3. Compute maximum bisections n from inequality (3)
4. Repeat n times
    4.1 Compute xM according to (2)
    4.2 If $f(xL).f(xM) > 0$ then
        4.2.1 Let xL = xM
        otherwise
        4.2.2 Let xR = xM
5. Print root xM
6. Stop

We have assumed that the method will not find the root exactly because of the minute chances of the equality comparison being true with real variables. But if you are skeptical, you can replace step 4 in the plan with a WHILE-WEND structure!

The next program uses the Bisection method to solve the equation discussed in the previous section.

```
100   REM BISECTION METHOD TO SOLVE F(X) = 0
110   DEF FNF( X ) = X ^ 3 + X – 3              'F(X)
120   READ XL, XR, EPS
130   NMAX = INT( LOG( ABS( XL – XR ) / EPS ) / LOG( 2 ) + 1 )
140
150   FOR I = 1 TO NMAX
160      XM = (XL + XR) / 2
170      IF FNF( XL ) * FNF( XM ) > 0 THEN XL = XM ELSE XR = XM
180      PRINT USING "#.######"; XM,
190      PRINT USING "  #.#### ^^^^"; FNF( XM )
200   NEXT I
210
220   DATA 1, 2, 1E-6
230   END
RUN
1.500000      0.1875E+01
1.250000      0.2031E+00
1.125000     –.4512E+00
1.187500     –.1379E+00
  .
  .
  .
1.213412      0.9537E–06
```

An advantage of the Bisection method is that it is guaranteed to find you a root if you can find the two starting values for xL and xR between which the function will change sign. You can also compute in advance the number of bisections needed to attain a given accuracy. Its disadvantage is that it is an inefficient method, in that successive bisections do not necessarily move closer to the root (e.g. the third bisection above), as generally happens with Newton's method. In fact, it is interesting to compare the two methods on the same function to see how many more steps the Bisection method requires than Newton's method. In the above example, for instance, the Bisection method takes 21 steps to reach the same accuracy that Newton's reaches in 5 steps.

14.2. Integration

Although almost all respectable mathematical functions can be differentiated analytically, the same cannot unfortunately be said for integration. There is no general rule for integrating, as there is for differentiating. (This is an interesting fact of mathematical life which you may wish to ponder!) For example, the indefinite integral of a function as simple as

$\exp(-x^2)$

cannot be found mathematically. We therefore need a numerical method for evaluating (definite) integrals.

This is actually quite easy to do, and depends on the well known fact that the definite integral of a function $f(x)$, say, between the limits $x = a$ and $x = b$, is equal to the area under f(x) bounded by the x-axis and the two lines $x = a$ and $x = b$. So all numerical methods for integrating simply involve more or less ingenious ways of estimating the area under f(x).

One rough and ready, yet perfectly valid, way of doing this is by drawing the curve f(x) on squared graph paper (the smaller the squares, the better) and counting the number of squares that fall under the curve. The only problem is what to do when the graph cuts across a square: do you count the square, or not, or how much of it do you count? The method that we will consider below, called the Trapezoidal Rule, or the Trapezium Rule, effectively approximates f(x) by a straight line across each square that it crosses, for the compelling reason that every schoolchild knows how to calculate the area of the resulting shape: a series of trapeziums.

14.2.1. The Trapezoidal Rule

Before we derive the rule, a little notation will make the problem clearer. We want to integrate f(x) with respect to x between the limits $x = a$ and $x = b$. We divide the area under f(x) up into a lot of vertical panels of equal width. The width of a panel is universally called h (and referred to as panel width, or step length, or grid size, or what have you), and for some reason there are always n of them. One such panel is shown in Figure 14-3.

Figure 14-3. A typical panel for the trapezoidal rule

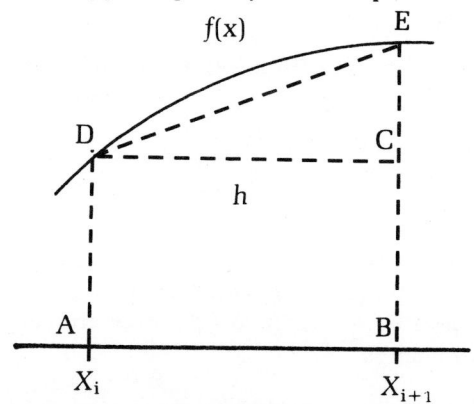

It should be fairly obvious then that, since a length $(b - a)$ of the x-axis has been cut up into n panels each of width h, h is given by

$$h = (b - a)/n,$$

or alternatively, n is given by

$$n = (b - a)/h.$$ (4)

The vertical edges of the panels will meet the x-axis at the points

$x = a; x = a + h; x = a + 2h; \ldots ; x = a + nh = b$.

We denote these points by $X_0, X_1, X_2, \ldots, X_n$, so that

$X_0 = a$

$X_1 = a + h$

$X_2 = a + 2h$

....

$X_i = a + ih$ (5)

....

$X_n = a + nh = b$.

If we draw a straight line across the top of each panel, from the point $(X_0; f(X_0))$ to $(X_1; f(X_1))$, and then to the point $(X_2; f(X_2))$, etc, we will have a set of n trapeziums, and we can approximate the area under f(x) by the area of these trapeziums.

One such trapezium is shown in Figure 14-3. The area of ABCDE is

$h(AD + BE)/2$,

i.e. $h[f(X_i) + f(X_i + h)]/2$.

The area we are after is the sum of all such trapeziums,

i.e. $\int_a^b f(x)dx$ is approximately equal to S, where S is given by

$S = 0.5h[f(X_0) + f(X_1)] + 0.5h[f(X_1) + f(X_2)] + ... + 0.5h[f(X_n - h) + f(X_n)]$

$= 0.5h[f(a) + f(b) + 2 \sum_{i=1}^{n-1} f(X_i)]$. (6)

Equ.(6) is the Trapezoidal Rule. As an example, we will write a program to evaluate the integral of

$f(x) = x^3$

between the limits $x = 0$ and $x = 4$. (The point of taking a function that we can integrate exactly is that we can check the accuracy of the numerical method. The exact answer here is 64.)

The following program computes the integral of any given function f(x) between the given limits a and b, using the Trapezoidal Rule with a panel width of h (also given). It is assumed that h will be chosen in such a way that n as defined in equ.(4) will be an integer.

```
100   REM INTEGRATION BY THE TRAPEZOIDAL RULE
110   DEF FNF( X ) = X ^ 3                    'INTEGRAND
120   READ A, B, H                            'LIMITS AND PANEL WIDTH
130   N = CINT( (B – A) / H )                 'N MUST BE AN INTEGER
140   SUM = 0                                 'THE INTEGRAL
150                                           '
155   FOR I = 1 TO N–1
160      SUM = SUM + FNF( A + I * H )         'USING EQU. 5
170   NEXT I
180                                           '
190   SUM = H / 2 * (FNF( A ) + FNF( B ) + 2 * SUM )
200   PRINT SUM
210                                           '
220   DATA 0, 4, 0.1
230   END
```

Note the use of the function CINT, which rounds to the nearest integer.

Table 14-1 shows the results obtained for some different values of h. It is clear that as h gets smaller, the estimated integral becomes more accurate.

Table 14-1. Effect of different steplengths

h	Integral (S)
1.00	68.0000
.50	65.0000
.10	64.0400
.01	64.0004

This example assumes that $f(x)$ is a continuous function which may be calculated at any x. In practice $f(x)$ could be points supplied as a result of an experiment. For example, the speed of an object $v(t)$ might be measured every so many seconds, and one might want to estimate the distance travelled as the area under the speed-time graph. The above program can still be used as long as one replaces the function FNF(X) by an array F(N) into which the experimental values have been read. The references to FNF(A), FNF(B), and FNF(A+I * H) in the program would also have to be replaced, by F(0), F(N), and F(I) respectively.

14.3. Numerical Differentiation

The Newton quotient for a general function $f(x)$ is given by

$$[f(x+h) - f(x)]/h, \qquad (*)$$

where h is "small". As h tends to zero, this quotient approaches the derivative df/dx. The Newton quotient may therefore be used to estimate a derivative numerically. It is a useful exercise to do this with a few well known functions to see how small you can make h before rounding errors cause problems (since expression (*) involves subtracting terms that eventually become equal when the limit of the computer's accuracy is reached). As an example, we use the Newton quotient to estimate $f'(x)$ for

$$f(x) = x^2$$

at x = 2, for various values of h (we know the exact answer is 4). The following program does this, and the results are shown in Table 14-2.

```
100 NUMERICAL DERIVATIVES THE NEWTON WAY
110 DEF FNF( X ) = X ^ 2
120 X = 2
130 H = 1
140 FOR I = 1 TO 8
150    DF = (FNF( X+H ) – FNF( X )) / H
160    PRINT USING "  ##.########"; H, DF
170    H = H / 10
180 NEXT I
190 END
```

Table 14-2. Estimates of $f'(x)$ for $f(x) = x^2$

h	$f'(x)$
1.00000000	5.00000000
.10000000	4.09999400
.01000000	4.01001000
.00100000	4.00066400
.00010000	3.99589600
.00001000	4.00543300
.00000100	3.81469800
.00000010	0.00000000

The results show that the best h for this particular problem is about 1E-3. But for h much smaller than this the estimate becomes totally unreliable. Generally, the best h for a given problem can only be found by trial and error. Finding it constitutes one of the major problems of numerical analysis.

14.4. First Order Differential Equations

The most interesting situations in real life that we may want to model, or represent quantitatively, are usually those in which the variables change in time (e.g. biological, electrical, and mechanical systems). If the changes are continuous then the system can often be represented with equations involving the derivatives of the variables. Such equations are called "differential equations". The main aim of a lot of modelling is to be able to write down a set of differential equations that describe the system being studied as accurately as possible. When one tries to "solve" these equations one usually runs into difficulties, because only a very small class of differential equations can be solved analytically. This is where numerical methods come in. We will consider only the simplest method of numerical solution in this section: Euler's Method.

To illustrate the method, we will take an example from Newtonian mechanics of motion under gravity against air resistance. Suppose a parachutist of mass 100 kg steps out of a stationary hovering helicopter, but neglects to open his parachute for 24 seconds. We would like to find his velocity as a function of time during this period. Assuming that air resistance cannot be neglected (ask any parachutist!), the man falls subject to two vertical forces: gravity acting downwards, and air resistance acting upwards. The air resistance force is assumed to be proportional to the square of his velocity (this is fairly accurate). Applying Newton's second law to the parachutist, we have

$$ma = mg - pv^2,$$

where m is his mass, a his downward acceleration, g the acceleration due to gravity (9.8 m/s^2), v his velocity, and p is a constant of proportionality. Dividing by m, we can rewrite this as

$$dv/dt = g - kv^2, \tag{1}$$

where $k = p/m$. Equ.(1) is the differential equation describing the motion of the parachutist under gravity. The constant k varies with shape and mass, and may be found experimentally from the "terminal velocity" of the falling object. This terminal velocity (vT) is reached when the object stops accelerating, and may be found by equating the RHS of equ.(1) to zero. Thus

$vT = \sqrt{g/k}$.

For a man of 100 kg, k is found to be about 0.004. Before we proceed with the numerical solution of equ.(1) we should note that this differential equation can be solved analytically, since it is of the type called variable separable. If you know about such things, you should be able to do the integration and show that

$v(t) = a[1 - \exp(-2akt)]/[1 + \exp(-2akt)]$, (2)

where a is a constant representing the terminal velocity, and we have used the fact that $v(0) = 0$ (the initial condition, deduced from the fact that the helicopter is stationary).

The basic problem to be overcome in trying to solve an equation like (1) numerically is the fact that a derivative (like dv/dt) can't be represented exactly on a digital computer, since the limit (h tends to zero, where h is a small increment in t) cannot be taken exactly. We therefore need to approximate the derivative, and we use the Newton quotient to do this.

14.4.1. Euler's Method

We now consider how to solve

$dv/dt = g - kv^2$ (1)

numerically for $0 < t \leq 24$ seconds (since the air resistance constant k will change when the parachute is opened at $t = 24$ seconds). Euler's method consists of replacing the derivative on the LHS of equ.(1) by its Newton quotient. If we do this, we get

$[v(t + h) - v(t)]/h = g - kv^2(t)$.

Making $v(t + h)$ the subject of the above equation results in

$v(t + h) = v(t) + h[g - kv^2(t)]$. (4)

The point about equ.(4) is that given v at some time t (like $t = 0$), we can compute v at time $t + h$. We can then replace $v(t)$ on the RHS of equ.(4) by the $v(t + h)$ we have just found, and get $v(t + 2h)$, and so on, until we have computed v over the whole time interval.

The only thing that isn't obvious about this exercise is what value to give h. Let's try $h = 2$ seconds. Then from equ.(4), starting at $t = 0$, we get

$v(2) = v(0) + 2[9.8 - 0.004 \times v^2(0)]$
$ = 0 + 2[9.8 - 0]$
$ = 19.6$ m/s (the exact value is 18.64 m/s).

We have integrated equ.(1) numerically from $t = 0$ to $t = 2$! Putting $v(2)$ into the RHS of equ.(4) we can now find $v(4)$:

$v(4) = v(2) + 2[9.8 - 0.004 \times 19.6^2]$
$ = 36.13$ m/s (exact: 32.64).

And again, $v(6)$ can now be computed:

$v(6) = v(4) + 2[9.8 - 0.004 \times 36.13^2]$
$\quad\quad = 45.29$ m/s (exact: 41.08).

We can go on like this as long as we like. In general, equ.(4) gives us Euler's rule for computing the next $v\dagger$ once we have v:

$$v\dagger = v + h[g - kv^2]. \tag{5}$$

It is very easy to write a program to do this, and then we can also test the accuracy of the numerical method by trying different values of h. The following program uses Euler's method as implemented in equ.(4) or (5) to compute v for the first 24 seconds of the parachutist's motion. Note that the FOR-NEXT loop has been generalized to cover 24 seconds whatever the value of h.

```
100   REM EULER'S (RHYMES WITH BOILER'S) METHOD
110   G = 9.8
120   READ K, H, T, V                              'AS DEFINED IN TEXT
130                                                '
140   FOR I = 1 TO 24/H
150     T = T + H
160     V = V + H * (G - K * V ^ 2)                'FROM EQU. 5
170     PRINT USING "  ##.##"; T, V
180   NEXT I
190                                                '
200   DATA 0.004, 0.5, 0, 0
210   END
```

Table 14-3 shows the results for $h = 2$ and $h = 0.5$, compared with the exact solution computed directly from equ.(2). We see from the table that the numerical solution is quite a lot better for the smaller of the two h values, the worst error being about 3%. We also see that the parachutist's terminal velocity (49.5 m/s) is correctly computed with both values of h. The errors in fact get less and less as t approaches 24 seconds.

Table 14-3. Euler's method on equ.(1)

Time (secs)	Velocity (m/s)		
	$h=2$	$h=0.5$	exact
2.0	19.60	18.94	18.64
4.0	36.13	33.45	32.64
6.0	45.29	42.00	41.08
8.0	48.48	46.22	45.50
10.0	49.28	48.11	47.65
12.0	49.45	48.92	48.65
14.0	49.49	49.26	49.11
16.0	49.50	49.40	49.32
18.0	49.50	49.46	49.42
20.0	49.50	49.48	49.46
22.0	49.50	49.49	49.48
24.0	49.50	49.49	49.49

Now let's see what happens when the man opens his parachute at $t = 24$ seconds. The air resistance term k will be different now: for an open parachute $k = 0.3$ is quite realistic. We can use the same program as before with a few minor changes, and obviously we need to supply new starting values for t and v: 24 and 49.49 respectively. Since $h = 0.5$ worked well last time, we try the same value now. The results are rather surprising:

Time	Velocity
24.5	−313.0
25.0	−15003.36
25.5	−33780130.00
26.0	−171164600000000.00

Not only does the man fly upwards: he also soon exceeds the speed of light! The results make nonsense physically: fortunately in this example our intuition tells us that something is wrong. The only remedy is to reduce h. Some experimenting will reveal that the results for $h = 0.01$ are much better. Some of these are shown in Table 14-4. It is instructive to examine why the method breaks down for $h = 0.5$ with the parachute open. Euler's method basically assumes that the derivative dv/dt (= acceleration) is constant during the interval h. The use of the Newton

Table 14-4. Parachute open ($h = 0.01$)

Time (secs)	Velocity (m/s)	
	Euler	Exact
24.01	42.24	43.18
24.02	36.99	38.32
24.03	32.98	34.46
24.04	29.81	31.32
24.05	27.25	28.72
24.06	25.12	26.53
24.07	23.32	24.67
24.08	21.79	23.06
24.09	20.46	21.66
24.10	19.30	20.43
24.20	12.69	13.32
24.30	9.85	10.24
24.40	8.34	8.60
24.50	7.45	7.62
24.60	6.88	7.01
24.70	6.51	6.60
24.80	6.27	6.33
24.90	6.10	6.15
25.00	5.98	6.02
25.50	5.76	5.77
26.00	5.72	5.73

quotient implies this. However, a glance at the correct results in Table 14-4 shows that this assumption doesn't hold over the period from $t = 24$ to $t = 24.5$ seconds. At the beginning of this interval there is an enormous deceleration of about 6 m/s² over a period of 0.01 seconds, whereas by the end of the first half second, the new terminal velocity has been nearly reached. The only way to correct the problem is to go on reducing h until the results seem reasonable. The principle is that h must be small enough to make the derivative approximately constant over the interval h.

Finally, we should note that Euler's method will be just as easy to compute if the air resistance term is not kv^2, but $kv^{1.8}$ (which is more accurate), although now an analytic solution cannot be found.

Euler's method in general

In general we want to solve a first order differential equation of the form

$$dy/dx = f(x,y), \qquad y(0) \text{ given.}$$

Euler's method replaces dy/dx by its Newton quotient, so the differential equation becomes

$$[y(x + h) - y(x)]/h = f(x,y). \tag{6}$$

Denoting $y(x)$ by y, and $y(x + h)$ by $y\dagger$, we can use equ.(6) to get $y\dagger$ in terms of y, starting with $y = y(0)$:

$$y\dagger = y + hf(x,y). \tag{7}$$

Equ.(7) is repeated, replacing y by $y\dagger$ each time, until we have computed y over the required range of integration.

14.4.2. Bacteria Growth

Euler's method performs quite adequately in the parachutist problem, once we have got the right value of h. In case you think that the numerical solution of all differential equations is just as easy, we will now consider an example where Euler's method doesn't do too well.

Suppose a colony of 1000 bacteria are multiplying at a rate of 0.8 per hour per individual (i.e. an individual produces an average of 0.8 offspring every hour). How many bacteria are there after 10 hours? Assuming that the colony grows continuously and without restriction, we can model this growth with the differential equation

$$dN/dt = 0.8N; \qquad N(0) = 1000; \tag{8}$$

where $N(t)$ is the population size at time t. This process is called "exponential growth", and equ.(8) may be solved exactly to give the well known formula for exponential growth:

$$N(t) = 1000 \exp(0.8t). \tag{9}$$

To solve equ.(8) numerically, we apply Euler's algorithm to it by replacing dN/dt with its Newton quotient, to get

$N(t + h) = N(t) + 0.8hN(t)$.

Using the notation of equ.(5), this can be written more concisely as

$N\dagger = N + 0.8hN$, (10)

where N takes the value of 1000 at time $t = 0$. Using equ.(10) we compute N for $t = 0$ to 10, replacing N by $N\dagger$ after each calculation. Taking $h = 0.5$ gives results depicted in Table 14-5, where the exact solution according to equ.(9) is also given.

This time the numerical solution is not too good. In fact the error gets worse at each step, and after 10 hours of bacteria time it is about 72%. Of course, the numerical solution will improve a little if we try h smaller, but there would still always be some value of t, however big, where the error exceeds some acceptable limit.

We may ask why Euler's method works so well with the parachutist, but so badly with the bacteria. The answer, as we mentioned earlier, lies in the type of numerical

Table 14-5. Bacteria growth ($h = 0.5$)

time	population		
(hours)	Euler	§14.4.3	exact
0.5	1400.	1480.	1492.
1.0	1960.	2190.	2226.
1.5	2744.	3242.	3320.
2.0	3842.	4798.	4953.
2.5	5378.	7101.	7389.
3.0	7530.	10509.	11023.
3.5	10541.	15554.	16445.
4.0	14758.	23019.	24533.
4.5	20661.	34069.	36598.
5.0	28925.	50422.	54598.
5.5	40496.	74624.	81451.
6.0	56694.	110444.	121510.
6.5	79371.	163457.	181272.
7.0	111120.	241916.	270426.
7.5	155568.	358035.	403428.
8.0	217795.	529892.	601845.
8.5	304913.	784240.	897847.
9.0	426879.	1160676.	1339429.
9.5	597630.	1717800.	1998194.
10.0	836683.	2542344.	2980955.

approximation to the derivative that is used. By using the Newton quotient each time in Euler's method, we are assuming that the derivative changes very little over the small interval h, i.e. that the SECOND derivative is very small. Now in the case of the parachutist, by differentiating equ.(1) again with respect to time, we see that the second derivative is

$-(2kv)dv/dt$,

which approaches zero as the object reaches its terminal velocity (since dv/dt approaches zero at terminal velocity). In the bacteria case, the second derivative of $N(t)$ is found by differentiating equ.(8). We get

$d^2N/dt^2 = 0.8 dN/dt = 0.8^2\, N(t)$.

This is far from zero at $t = 10$. In fact, it is approaching two million! Therefore the Newton quotient approximation gets worse at each step in this case.

There are better numerical methods for overcoming these sorts of problems. Two of them are discussed below. More sophisticated methods may be found in any textbook on numerical analysis. However, Euler's method may always be used as a first approximation as long as you realise where and why errors may arise.

14.4.3. A Predictor Corrector Method

One improvement on the solution of

$dy/dx = f(x,y)$, $y(0)$ given,

is as follows. Euler says compute

$y\dagger = y + hf(x,y)$ (7)

repeatedly. But this way favours the old value of y in computing $f(x,y)$ on the RHS. Surely it would be better to say

$y\dagger = y + h[f(x + h, y\dagger) + f(x,y)]/2$,   (11)

since this also involves the new value $y\dagger$ in computing f on the RHS. The problem is that $y\dagger$ is as yet unknown, so we can't use it on the RHS of equ.(11). But we could use Euler to estimate (predict) $y\dagger$ from equ.(7) and then use equ.(11) to correct the prediction by computing a better version of $y\dagger$, say y^*. So the full procedure is:

1. Use Euler to predict

    $y\dagger = y + hf(x,y)$

2. Then correct $y\dagger$ as follows:

    $y^* = y + h[f(x + h, y\dagger) + f(x,y)]/2$

3. Replace y by y^* in step (1) and repeat.

This is called a "Predictor Corrector" method. It can be applied to the bacteria growth problem as follows, and only requires one extra line in the computer program:

$N\dagger = N + 0.8hN$ (predictor: as before),

$N^* = N + 0.8h(N\dagger + N)/2$ (corrector).

The results using this method are also shown in Table 14-5, where the worst error has now been reduced to 15%. This is much better than the uncorrected Euler algorithm, although there is still much room for improvement.

14.5. Runge-Kutta Methods

There are a variety of formulae, under the general name of Runge-Kutta, of varying degrees of accuracy, which can be used to integrate almost any system of ordinary differential equations. The "third-order" formula is given here, for reference. A derivation of this and the other Runge-Kutta formulae can be found in most books on numerical analysis.

14.5.1. Runge-Kutta Third Order Formula

The general differential equation is

$dy/dx = f(x,y),$ $y(0)$ given.   (*)

The value of y at $x = h$ is then given by

$y\dagger = y + (k_1 + 4k_2 + k_3)/6$

where

$k_1 = hf(x,y)$
$k_2 = hf(x + 0.5h, y + 0.5k_1)$
$k_3 = hf(x + h, y + 2k_2 - k_1)$

14.5.2. A Predator Prey Model

The Runge-Kutta formulae may be adapted to integrate systems of differential equations. Here we use the third-order formulae to integrate the well known predator prey system,

$dx/dt = f(x,y) = px - qxy$
$dy/dt = g(x,y) = rxy - sy$

where $x(t)$ and $y(t)$ are the prey and predator populations respectively at time t, and p, q, r and s are biologically determined parameters. In this case, the values of x and y at some time t may be used to find $x\dagger$ and $y\dagger$ at time $t + h$ with the formulae

$x\dagger = x + (k_1 + 4k_2 + k_3) / 6$
$y\dagger = y + (m_1 + 4m_2 + m_3) / 6$

where

$k_1 = hf(x, y)$
$m_1 = hg(x, y)$
$k_2 = hf(x + 0.5k_1, y + 0.5m_1)$
$m_2 = hg(x + 0.5k_1, y + 0.5m_1)$
$k_3 = hf(x + 2k_2 - k_1, y + 2m_2 - m_1)$
$m_3 = hg(x + 2k_2 - k_1, y + 2m_2 - m_1)$

It should be noted that in this example x and y are the dependent variables and t (which does not appear explicitly in the equations) is the independent variable, whereas in the general formula (*) quoted in the previous section, y is the dependent variable, and x is the independent variable.

The next program implements this scheme for the predator prey model, taking $h = 1$ year, $x(0) = 105$, $y(0) = 8$, $p = 0.4$, $q = 0.04$, $r = 0.02$, and $s = 2$. The output shows the characteristic cyclic behaviour of the two populations (with a period in this case of 7 years: different parameters will change the period).

```
100   REM RUNGE-KUTTA FOR PREDATOR PREY MODEL
110   DEF FNF( X, Y ) = P * X - Q * X * Y         'RHS OF PREY EQU.
120   DEF FNG( X, Y ) = R * X * Y - S * Y         'RHS OF PRED EQU.
130                                               '
140   READ P, Q, R, S                             'PARAMETERS
150   READ X, Y                                   'INITIAL VALUES
160   READ H                                      'STEP LENGTH
170
180   CLS
190   FOR T = H TO 40 STEP H
200      GOSUB 500
210      PRINT USING "#####."; T, X, Y
220   NEXT T
230
240   DATA 0.4, 0.04, 0.02, 2
250   DATA 105, 8
260   DATA 1
270   END
280
500   REM 3RD ORDER RUNGE-KUTTA FOR TWO 1ST ORDER DEs
510   K1 = H * FNF( X, Y )
520   M1 = H * FNG( X, Y )
530   K2 = H * FNF( X + K1 / 2, Y + M1 / 2 )
540   M2 = H * FNG( X + K1 / 2, Y + M1 / 2 )
550   K3 = H * FNF( X + 2 * K2 - K1, Y + 2 * M2 - M1 )
560   M3 = H * FNG( X + 2 * K2 - K1, Y + 2 * M2 - M1 )
570
580   REM NOW UPDATE X AND Y OVER ONE TIME STEP
590   X = X + (K1 + 4 * K2 + K3) / 6
600   Y = Y + (M1 + 4 * M2 + M3) / 6
610
620   RETURN
RUN
        1    111   10
        2    108   12
        3     98   12
        4     91   11
        5     91    9
        6     97    8
        7    105    8
        8    110   10
        9    106   12
       10     98   12
       11     92   11
       12     93    9
       13     98    8
       14    105    9
       ....
```

14.6. EXERCISES

14.1 Write down Newton's algorithm to find the cube root of 2. Taking 1.0 as the starting value, use a calculator to do the first few iterations, and observe how fast they converge.

14.2 Use Newton's method in a program to solve some of the following (you may have to experiment a bit with the starting value):

(a) $x^4 - x = 10$ (two real roots)

(b) $\exp(-x) = \sin(x)$ (infinitely many roots)

(c) $x^3 - 8x^2 + 17x - 10 = 0$ (three real roots)

(d) $\log(x) = \cos(x)$

(e) $x^4 - 5x^3 - 12x^2 + 76x - 79 = 0$ (find the two roots near 2)

14.3 Use the Bisection method by hand to find the square root of 2, taking 1.0 and 2.0 as initial values for xL and xR. Continue bisecting until the maximum error is less than 0.05 (use equ.(3) of §14.1 to determine how many bisections are needed).

14.4 Use the trapezoidal rule by hand to evaluate

$$\int_0^4 x^2 \, dx,$$ using a step-length of $h = 1.0$.

14.5 Consider the differential equation

$dx/dt = 1 - x, \quad x(0) = 0.$

Use Euler's method by hand to estimate x(1), using (a) two steps of length $h = 0.5$, and (b) four steps of length $h = 0.25$.

14.6 Use Euler's method by hand to evaluate the integral in Ex. 14.4 using the same step-length.

14.7 A human population N of 1000 at time $t = 0$ grows at a rate given by $dN/dt = aN$, where $a = 0.025$ per year per person. Use the Euler Method to predict the population over the next 30 years:

(i) working in steps $h = 2$ years
(ii) working in steps $h = 1$ year
(iii) working in steps $h = 0.5$ years.

Compare your answers with the exact mathematical solution.

14.8 Radio-active substance A decays into substance B at a rate given by the equation

$dx/dt = -rx$

where x is the amount (in kg) of A present at time t, and r is a constant called the decay-rate.

(a) Solve for x as a function of time (analytically).
(b) Show that the initial amount of A present is reduced by a half in time

$T = 0.693/r$. (T is the half-life of A).

(c) If y is the amount of B present at time t, and if $y = 0$, at time $t = 0$, deduce an expression for y as a function of time.

(d) Given $r = 0.0033$ per year and $x = 10$ kg at time $t = 0$, use the Euler Method to find x as a function of time for a period of 450 years. Work in steps of $h = 15$ years and compare answers with the exact solution.

14.9 Some radio-active substances decay into other radio-active substances which in turn also decay. For example, Strontium 92 ($r_1 = 0.256$ per hr) decays into Yttrium 92 ($r_2 = 0.127$ per hr) which in turn decays into Zirconium. Write down a pair of simultaneous differential equations to describe what is happening.

Starting with 5.E26 atoms of Strontium 92, use the Euler method to solve the equations up to $t = 8$ hours in steps of $1/3$ hr.

14.10 Solve numerically $y' = x - y$ over the domain [0; 1] using $h = 0.2$ and $y(0) = 1$.

14.11 The impala population $x(t)$ in the Kruger National Park may be modelled by the equation

$dx/dt = [r - bx\ sin(\omega t)]x$,

where r, b, and ω are constants. Write a program which reads values for r, b, and ω, and initial values for x and t, and which uses Euler's method to compute the impala population at monthly intervals over a period of two years.

APPENDIX A

PROGRAMMING STYLE

A program which is written any old how, although it may do what is required, is going to be difficult to understand when you go through it again after a month or two, particularly if you want to make some changes to it. Serious programmers therefore pay a fair amount of attention to what is called programming style, in order to make their programs clearer and more readable both to themselves, and to other potential users. You may find this irritating, if you are starting to program for the first time, because you are naturally impatient to get on with the job. But a little extra attention to your program layout will pay enormous dividends in the long run, especially when it comes to debugging!

Some hints on how to improve your programming style are given below (the example in §4.2 gives a good idea of what is meant by programming style).

1) You should make liberal use of comments (REM and inline) both at the beginning of the program or subroutines, to describe briefly what the program does and any special methods that have been used (e.g. Euler's Method for numerical integration), and also throughout the program to introduce various logical sections. Any restrictions on the size and type of data that may be used as input should be stated clearly (e.g. maximum size of a matrix).

2) You should describe briefly the function of each variable in comments (in alphabetical order) at the beginning of the program.

3) Blank lines should be used to separate logical sections of the coding.

4) Coding inside FOR-NEXT loops should be indented a few columns to make the logical structure more apparent.

5) Blanks should be used in statements in the following places:
   — on either side of arithmetic or logical operators;
   — on either side of the '=' symbol in assignment statements;
   — after all commas;
   — on either side of argument lists in functions.

   However, blanks can be omitted in places in complex expressions, where this may make the structure clearer, e.g.

   IF B^2 < 4*A*C THEN PRINT "ROOTS ARE IMAGINARY"

6) The GOTO statement should only be used in the IF–GOTO conditional repeat structure, as outlined in §5.4, and then only if your version of BASIC does not have the WHILE-WEND statements.

APPENDIX B

SUMMARY OF BASIC STATEMENTS

This appendix contains a working summary of Microsoft BASIC statements. You should consult your computer's manual for the full treatment. In all the statements below, square brackets [ ] denote optional arguments (i.e. the square brackets should never be typed literally).

BEEP

blows the hooter, at a frequency of 800 Hz for 0.25 seconds. It has the same effect as

PRINT CHR$(7);

CHAIN

transfers control to a program stored on a diskette, and runs it after passing certain variables to it from the current program. In general

CHAIN [MERGE] FILENAME [, [line] [, [ALL] [, DELETE range]]]

where "line" is the line number from where the chained program must start running. The default value is the first line in the program.

ALL specifies that every variable (with its current value) must be passed from the current program to the chained program, e.g.

CHAIN "TEST", 500, ALL

If ALL is omitted, no variables are passed. In that case the COMMON statement may be used to pass some variables.

MERGE brings the named program into memory as an overlay, i.e. without erasing the current contents. The chained program must be an ASCII file if MERGE is used. You may wish to delete part of the memory to make room for the overlay, and this is done with the DELETE option, e.g.

CHAIN MERGE "TEST", 1000, DELETE 1000–5000

This will delete lines 1000–5000 of the current program before bringing in the overlay, which starts running at line 1000.

CIRCLE

draws a circle of given specifications, e.g.

CIRCLE (x, y), r [, colour [, start, end]]

draws a circle of radius r centred at the point (x; y), of given colour. Partial arcs may be drawn by specifying "start" and "end" in radians between -2 π and 2 π.

CLOSE

closes the specified files, e.g.

CLOSE [#1, #2, ...]

closes files number 1, 2, etc. The default position is that all files are closed.

CLS

clears the screen and places the cursor in the "home" position: at the top lefthand corner. This has the same effect as pressing **Ctrl/Home.**

COLOR (Graphics)

selects the colours to be used in graphics mode. The general form is

COLOR background, palette

where "background" is a number in the range 0 to 15 that selects the background colour, as described in COLOR (Text), and "palette" is either 0 or 1, and selects the colour palette. The palettes available in medium resolution graphics, and the codes for their four colours, are as follows:

Palette Code	Colour Code	Meaning
0	0	background
	1	green
	2	red
	3	yellow
1	0	background
	1	blue
	2	magenta
	3	white

COLOR (Text)

selects the colours for the text screen as follows:

COLOR [foreground] [, [background] [, border]]

where "foreground" is the colour of the text, and "background" is the part of the screen not covered with text and not included in the "border" around the edge of the screen.

The following colours are available:

Colour Code	Meaning
0	black
1	blue
2	green
3	cyan

4	red
5	magenta
6	brown
7	white
8	gray
9	light blue
10	light green
11	light cyan
12	light red
13	light magenta
14	yellow
15	bright white

If 16 is added to a foreground colour code, the character blinks.

COMMON

passes variables through to a chained program and is used in conjunction with the CHAIN statement:

COMMON list of variables separated by commas.

There may be more than one COMMON statement in a program, but it is recommended that they all appear together at the beginning of the program. A variable may not be listed in more than one COMMON. Any array names that are passed must have "()" appended, and do not need to be re-dimensioned in the chained program. E.g.,

10   COMMON MARK(), NAM$(), TOP

DATA

contains the data (string or numeric constants) for a READ statement:

DATA list of constants separated by commas.

The constants are assigned in order to the variables in READs. All the constants in all DATA statements in a program may be thought of as a continuous list of items which are accessed sequentially by successive READs through the program. The items in a DATA statement may be re-read by using the RESTORE statement.

String constants in DATA need not be enclosed in quotes unless the string contains embedded commas or colons, or significant leading and trailing blanks. See Chapter Two for examples.

DEF FN

defines and names a one-line function of your own choice:

DEF FNname (arguments) = expression

The same rules for variable names apply to the suffix "name", which has a type (integer, string, etc.) specified in the usual way. The arguments are dummy variables, i.e. they are used only to define the function, and will not be confused with variables of the same name elsewhere in the program.

DEFtype

where "type" may be INT, SNG, DBL or STR respectively, specifies the variables starting with the listed letters with the appropriate type. E.g.,

```
10  DEFINT I-N, Z
20  DEFSTR A, E
```

specifies variables starting with the letters I to N inclusive, and Z, with type integer, and those starting with the letters A and E with type string. However, a type declaration character (%, !, #, or $) always takes precedence over a DEFtype statement.

DIM

dimensions an array. The maximum number of dimensions per array is 255, and the maximum number of elements per dimension is 32767. The minimum value of subscripts is zero by default, but this may be overruled by the OPTION BASE statement.

DRAW

draws a figure of any specified shape on the screen. The general form is

DRAW "command string"

where the command string is a string variable or constant containing various command codes as described below. E.g.,

DRAW "R10U10L10D10"

draws a box of side 10 points, so that the bottom left corner of the box is where the current position was before the statement was executed.
The draw commands are executed from left to right in the string, and move the current point a given number of steps, drawing an image while doing so. To get this right, it is best to draw the image required on squared graph paper before getting thoroughly tangled up. The possible commands are as follows:

Command	Meaning
Un	move UP n points
Dn	move DOWN n points
Ln	move LEFT n points
Rn	move RIGHT n points
En	move diagonally: up n points and right n points
Fn	move diagonally: down n points and right n points
Gn	move diagonally: down n points and left n points
Hn	move diagonally: up n points and left n points
Cc	set image colour to colour code c

A more general draw command is

Mp,q

which moves the current point to the position with co-ordinates (p; q). If p or q are unsigned digits they specify absolute co-ordinates. However, if either is preceded by a + or − sign, the movement is relative to the current position.

The prefix B before any draw command inhibits drawing: the current position becomes the position specified, but without drawing an image on the way.

The prefix N returns the current position to the original position after drawing.

END

terminates execution, closes all files, and returns to command (direct) level.

ERASE

eliminates arrays from a program (in order to reclaim memory space). E.g.,

ERASE NAM$, MARKS

will erase the listed arrays.

FOR and NEXT

are used to execute repeatedly the set of statements enclosed between FOR and NEXT, e.g.

```
10   FOR I = 10 TO 3 STEP -2
20      PRINT I;
30   NEXT I
RUN
10  8  6  4
```

See §5.5.3 for the full definition.

GET (Graphics)

reads an image from a given area of the screen, e.g.

GET (x1, y1) − (x2, y2), array

where (x1; y1) and (x2; y2) are the opposite corners of the rectangular area of the screen to be stored in "array", which must be suitably dimensioned. The image thus stored may be subsequently drawn on the screen with the PUT statement.

GOSUB and RETURN

branch to and return from the subroutine starting at the given line number. See Chapter Four for examples.

GOTO

branches unconditionally to the specified line number. It is considered bad programming style to use GOTO under any circumstances other than the IF-GOTO conditional repeat structure outlined in Chapter Five!

To maintain a high standard of programming style you should never use GOTO if you have WHILE-WEND in your version of BASIC!

IF

executes statements conditionally depending on the logical value of an expression:

IF expression THEN s1 [ELSE s2]

If "expression" is true, statement s1 is executed. Otherwise statement s2 is executed (if the ELSE clause is present).

INPUT

receives input from the keyboard during program execution:

INPUT [;] ["prompt";] list of variables separated by commas

or

INPUT [;] ["prompt",] list of variables separated by commas

In the second form, the question mark prompt is suppressed, e.g.

10   INPUT "NAME:", N$
RUN
NAME:©

where © indicates the position of the cursor. See §2.3 for more examples.

INPUT

reads data from the file with given number:

INPUT #filenumber, list of variables separated by commas

This works for input from files exactly as INPUT works for input from the keyboard, except that prompts are not displayed on the screen. The file being read must have been opened for input, and is then regarded as a sequential file. E.g.,

10   INPUT #1, NAM$, MARK

KEY

may be used to switch on and off the display of "soft keys" at the bottom of the screen. KEY OFF switches the display off. KEY ON switches it on again.

LINE

draws a straight line on the screen between two given points. There are two particularly useful forms of this statement. The first is

LINE − (x, y), colour

which draws a line from the current position to the point (x; y) in the specified colour. The second is

LINE (x1, y1) − (x2, y2), colour

which draws a line from (x1; y1) to (x2; y2) in the specified colour. Another form of the statement is

LINE (x1, y1) − (x2, y2), colour, B[F]

which draws a rectangle with corners (x1; y1) and (x2; y2). The rectangle is filled in with the given colour if the F option is used.

LINE INPUT

reads an entire line (up to 254 characters) from the keyboard into a string variable, ignoring commas:

LINE INPUT [;] ["prompt";] string variable

The question mark prompt is not printed unless it is part of the "prompt" string. E.g.,

```
10  LINE INPUT V$
20  PRINT V$
RUN
1,2,3,4,®
1,2,3,4,
```

LINE INPUT

reads from the given sequential file as LINE INPUT reads from the keyboard. It reads all the characters in the current line of the file up to the next carriage return.

LOCATE

positions the cursor (which may be turned on or off) on the screen. Its simplest form is:

LOCATE row, col, cursor

"Row" must have the value 1 to 25, to give the vertical position of the cursor (1 is at the top of the screen). "Column" must be in the range 1 to 40 or 1 to 80, depending on your screen width, and gives the horizontal position of the cursor. "Cursor" switches the cursor on (1) or off (0). E.g., the following program will print an oval on the screen:

```
100 G$ = "*"
110   CLS
120   R = 8
130   SC = 2
140   PI = 3.141593
150   CY = 12.5
160   CX = 40
170   FOR ANG = 0 TO 2*PI STEP PI/40
180     Y = R * SIN( ANG )
190     X = R * COS( ANG ) * SC
200     LOCATE CY + Y, CX + X
210     PRINT G$
220   NEXT ANG
230   END
```

LPRINT

sends output to the printer. It works exactly like PRINT, except that the number of print zones on a line differs. LPRINT may be used with special control characters to change the dot matrix printing characteristics (e.g. bold, underlined, 12 point, etc.). The manual that goes with your computer system's printer should have the details.

LPRINT USING

works just like PRINT USING, except that output is sent to the printer.

ON TIMER

transfers control to a given line number after a given number of seconds has elapsed:

ON TIMER(s) GOSUB m

This must be used in conjuction with a TIMER ON statement to activate it. E.g.,

```
10  ON TIMER( 60 ) GOSUB 1000
20  TIMER ON
.
.
```

Every 60 seconds GOSUB 1000 is executed. This can be used to print the time regularly on the screen, for example. The TIMER OFF statement later in the program de-activates ON TIMER.

OPEN

allows sequential files to be used for input, output or appending. E.g.,

```
10  OPEN "F1" FOR INPUT AS #1
20  OPEN "F2" FOR OUTPUT AS #2
30  OPEN "F3" FOR APPEND AS #3
```

An INPUT #1 statement then reads from F1, PRINT #2 or WRITE #2 or PRINT #2 USING will write to F2 (destroying the previous contents), while PRINT #3 or WRITE #3 or PRINT #3 USING will append on the end of the current contents of F3.

The first two of these statements may be written in an alternative form:

```
10  OPEN "O", #1, "F1"
20  OPEN "I", #2, "F2"
```

OPTION BASE

declares the minimum subscript values for arrays. By default this is zero, but the statement

```
10  OPTION BASE 1
```

sets the minimum subscript value to one. The OPTION BASE statement must appear in the program before any DIM statements.

PAINT

fills an area of the screen with a given colour. The statement is as follows:

PAINT (x, y), paint, border

Painting starts at the point (x; y) with the colour "paint", and covers the area bounded by a figure drawn with colour "border".

PRINT

displays data on the screen:

PRINT list of expressions

where the expressions may be string or numeric constants, and must be separated by blanks, commas, semi-colons, or TAB statements. The list may be terminated with a comma or semi-colon. The screen is divided into print zones of 14 spaces each. A comma after an item in the print list causes the next item to be printed in the next print zone: a semi-colon leaves one or two blanks before the next item, depending on whether or not it has a minus sign.

A trailing comma or semi-colon at the end of the print list causes the next PRINT statement further on in the program to continue printing on the same line.

One or more blanks between items in the list has the same effect as a semi-colon. E.g.,

```
10   N$ = "XYZ"
20   A = 1: B = -2: C = 3
30   PRINT N$; A B; "C=", C
RUN
XYZ 1 -2 C=        3
```

PRINT USING

prints strings or numbers on the screen using a specified format:

PRINT USING v$; list of expressions [;]

where v$ is a string constant or variable consisting of special formatting characters which determine how the list of expressions will be printed. PRINT USING is discussed in detail in Chapter Eight, but a brief example is also given below:

```
10   X = 123.345
20   PRINT USING "X: ####.#b"; X, X,
30   PRINT USING "#.### ^^^^"; X
40   PRINT USING "      "; "ABCDEF"
RUN
X:    123.5bX:    123.5b0.123E+03
ABC
```

PRINT

writes data sequentially to a file which has been opened for output or append:

PRINT #filenum, list of expressions

where "filenum" is the file number used in the corresponding OPEN statement. PRINT # makes an image of the data in the file exactly as it would appear on the screen. PRINT # is discussed in detail in Chapter Eight.

PRINT # USING

writes data sequentially to a file according to a specified format:

PRINT #filenum, USING v$; list of expressions

This statement sends an image of the data to the file exactly as it would appear on the screen.

PSET

draws a dot at the given position:

PSET(x, y) [, colour]

PUT (Graphics)

displays a graphic image, previously stored with GET, at a specified position on the screen. The general form is

PUT (x, y), array [, operation]

where (x; y) are the co-ordinates of the upper left corner of the rectangular area of the screen in which the image, previously stored in "array", will be displayed.

"Operation" specifies what must be done with points already on the screen in the image area. For example, the operation OR displays the graphic image overlapping points already there, whereas XOR negates points already there. XOR (which is the default operation) may therefore be used for animation (see §12.2.3).

RANDOMIZE

reseeds the random number generator RND. If used in conjunction with the TIMER function, a different seed for RND is generated each time the program is run, thus ensuring that RND returns a different random number sequence each time, e.g.

10 RANDOMIZE TIMER

See Chapter Ten for examples.

READ

reads values from a DATA statement and assigns them in sequence to the variables listed in the READ:

READ list of variables separated by commas

READ must be used in conjunction with a DATA statement. A single READ may access more than one DATA statement, or several READs may access the same DATA statement, the next READ taking up where the last one left off. See §2.7 for examples.

RESTORE

allows DATA statements to be reread from a given line:

RESTORE [line]

where "line" is the line number of the DATA statement from where the reread is to begin.

RETURN

transfers control back to the line following a GOSUB statement, with which RETURN should always be used.

SCREEN

selects the screen mode, as follows

SCREEN n

where n has the following effects:

0: text (40 or 80 characters per line);
1: medium resolution graphics (320 x 200 points);
2: high resolution graphics (640 x 200 points).

SOUND

generates sound through the speaker:

SOUND freq, duration

where "freq" is the desired frequency in Hertz (cycles per second), in the range 37 to 32767, and "duration" is the desired duration in clock ticks. The IBM clock ticks 18.2 times per second. "Duration" must be a numeric expression in the range 0 to 65535.

The note A below middle C has a frequency of 440. Middle C therefore has a frequency of 523.25. E.g.,

10   SOUND 261.63, 36.4

plays C below middle C for two seconds.

STOP

terminates execution and returns to command level with a message

Break in n

where n is the line number where the STOP occurs.

SWAP

exchanges the values of two variables:

SWAP var1, var2

Variables of any type may be swapped, but they must both be of the same type. Array elements may also be swapped. This saves coding in a Bubble sort, for example.

WHILE and WEND

executes a series of statements while a given condition is true:

n WHILE expression

.
.

m WEND

where expression is any numeric or logical expression. The statements between WHILE and WEND are repeatedly executed, but only while "expression" is true (not zero). WHILE-WEND loops may be nested.

In the following example, the series 1 + 2 + 3 + ... is summed until the sum is the highest integer not exceeding 100. This highest value is printed, with the last member of the series used:

```
10   SUM = 0
20   I = 0
30   WHILE SUM < 100
40     ANS = SUM
50     I = I + 1
60     SUM = SUM + I
70   WEND
80   PRINT I−1; ANS
RUN
 13    91
```

WIDTH

sets the width of the screen or printer in number of characters. For the screen, the form is

WIDTH n

where n may only take the values 40 or 80. This statement is necessary, together with SCREEN 0, to revert to 80-column text mode mode after using medium resolution graphics. For the printer, the form is

WIDTH "LPT1:", n

where n is the number of characters to be printed per line.

WRITE

outputs data to the screen, inserting commas between items, and enclosing strings in quotes, e.g.

```
10   N$ = "SMITH"
20   M1 = 10
30   M2 = 0
40   M3 = 98.4
50   WRITE N$, M1, M2, M3
RUN
"SMITH",10,0,98.4
```

WRITE

writes data to a sequential file in the same way that WRITE prints on the screen, e.g.

```
50   WRITE #1, N$, M1, M2, M3
```

APPENDIX C

SUMMARY OF BASIC COMMANDS

Commands differ from statements in the sense that they involve the operating system rather than programming instructions. Commands may also, however, be programmed, and may therefore appear as valid statements in a program. The following is a list of the more commonly used commands supported by Microsoft BASIC.

AUTO

generates line numbers automatically for program entry:

AUTO [n] [, m]

where n is the line number from where generation begins, and m is the increment. The default values of n and m are both 10. If a line number is generated which already exists in the workspace, an asterisk is displayed next to the line number to warn you.
To de-activate AUTO, press **Ctrl/Break.**

For example

AUTO

generates line numbers 10, 20, 30, ..., while

AUTO 100, 5

generates line numbers 100, 105, 110, ...

CLEAR

sets all numeric variables to zero and all string variables to null (as opposed to blank).

CONT

resumes execution after a break caused by STOP, END, an error, or by pressing **Ctrl/Break.**

DELETE

deletes program lines:

DELETE n-m

In this form lines n to m inclusive are deleted. If either of lines n or m does not exist, an "Illegal function call" error occurs. If -m is omitted, only line n is deleted. If m is omitted, then all lines from n onward are deleted. If n is omitted, then all lines from the beginning of the program up to and including line m are deleted. E.g.

DELETE 100-150

deletes lines 100 to 150 inclusive,

DELETE 25

deletes line 25 only, and

DELETE 200-

deletes from line 200 to the end of the program.

EDIT

displays a line for editing, e.g.

EDIT 250

displays line 250 and positions the cursor at the beginning of the line ready for editing.

FILES

displays the names of files on the diskette in drive A. To display the directory of the diskette in drive B, use the form

FILES "B:"

KILL

deletes a file from a diskette. The extension of the filename (.BAS in the case of BASIC program files) must be supplied. E.g.

KILL "RUBBISH.BAS"   (file on diskette in Drive A)
KILL "B:PLONK.BAS"   (file on diskette in Drive B)

LIST

lists (part of) the program currently in memory:

LIST n-m

Lines n to m inclusive will be listed. If -m is omitted, only line n is listed. If m is omitted, all the lines from n to the end of the program are listed. If n is omitted, all the lines from the beginning of the program up to and including line m are listed. If n-m is omitted, the whole program is listed. For example,

LIST 120-150

will list lines 120 to 150 inclusive.

LLIST

works exactly like LIST except that the lines are printed on the printer. It may be suspended with **Ctrl/Break.**

LOAD

loads a program from a diskette into memory and optionally runs it:

SUMMARY OF BASIC COMMANDS

LOAD "FILENAME" [, R]

For example,

LOAD "PLONK"

loads a program from the diskette in Drive A.

LOAD "B:TEST", R

loads a program from the diskette in Drive B and executes it.

MERGE

merges (overlays) the lines from an ASCII program file into the program currently in memory, e.g.

MERGE "PLONK"

The program file must have been saved as an ASCII file, i.e. with the A option under SAVE.

NAME

changes the name of a file on a diskette, e.g.

NAME "OLDONE" AS "NEWONE"

The file "OLDONE" must exist on the diskette, and the file "NEWONE" must not exist.

NEW

deletes the program currently in memory, and clears all variables.

RENUM

renumbers the program lines in memory:

RENUM [new] [, [old] [,incr]]

where "new" is the first line number to be used in the renumbered sequence, "old" is the line in the current program where renumbering is to begin, and "incr" is the increment to be used in the new sequence. The defaults are 10, from the beginning of the program. E.g.

RENUM 100

renumbers the whole program so that the first line is 100.

RENUM 500, 250

renumbers from 250 onwards to start at 500 with an increment of 10.
RENUM cannot be used to change the order of the program lines.

RESET

closes all files and clears the system buffer.

RUN

executes the program in memory. It has two forms:

RUN [n]
RUN "FILENAME"

In the first form, execution begins from line n (the beginning of the program by default). Running from a given line number is useful when developing a program. In the second form, the program specified is loaded from the diskette and executed.

SAVE

saves a program on a diskette. There are two forms:

SAVE "FILENAME" [, A]
SAVE "FILENAME", P

In the first form the program is saved (by default in compressed binary, which is the usual way, since it saves space) and can be subsequently loaded, executed and listed. If the saved program is to be merged, the A (ASCII) option must be used.

In the second form, the program is saved in an encoded binary form as protection against being illegally copied. When a protected program is loaded, it can be run, but not listed or edited. There is no way to unprotect a protected program.

SYSTEM

exits from BASIC and returns to DOS (the Disk Operating System).

TRON and TROFF

trace the execution of program statements. E.g.

TRON

switches the trace on. Subsequent RUNs cause the line numbers of the program to be printed in order of execution. This is a useful debugging aid. The trace remains in operation until the command TROFF is issued.

APPENDIX D

RESERVED WORDS

The following list of keywords are reserved and may not be used as variable names. Type declaration characters (%, !, $, #) may not be appended either. E.g. NAME$ may not be used as a string variable name since NAME is reserved, being a command.

ABS, AND, ASC, ATN, AUTO

BEEP, BLOAD, BSAVE

CALL, CDBL, CHAIN, CHDIR, CHR$, CINT, CIRCLE, CLEAR, CLOSE, CLS, COLOR, COM, COMMON, CONT, COS, CSNG, CSRLIN, CVD, CVI, CVS

DATA, DATE$, DEF, DEFDBL, DEFINT, DEFSNG, DEFSTR, DELETE, DIM, DRAW

EDIT, ELSE, END, ENVIRON, ENVIRON$, EOF, EQV, ERASE, ERDEV, ERDEV$, ERL, ERR, ERROR, EXP

FIELD, FILES, FIX, FNxxxx..., FOR, FRE

GET, GOSUB, GOTO

HEX$

IF, IMP, INKEY$, INP, INPUT, INPUT#, INPUT$, INSTR, INT, INTER$, IOCTL, IOCTL$

KEY, KEY$, KILL

LEFT$, LEN, LET, LINE, LIST, LLIST, LOAD, LOC, LOCATE, LOF, LOG, LPOS, LPRINT, LSET

MERGE, MID$, MKDIR, MKD$, MKI$, MKS$, MOD, MOTOR

NAME, NEW, NEXT, NOT

OCT$, OFF, ON, OPEN, OPTION, OR, OUT

PAINT, PEEK, PEN, PLAY, PMAP, POINT, POKE, POS, PRESET, PRINT, PRINT#, PSET, PUT

RANDOMIZE, READ, REM, RENUM, RESET, RESTORE, RESUME, RETURN, RIGHT$, RMDIR, RND, RSET, RUN

SAVE, SCREEN, SGN, SHELL, SIN, SOUND, SPACE$, SPC(, SQR, STEP, STICK, STOP, STR$, STRIG, STRING$, SWAP, SYSTEM

TAB(, TAN, THEN, TIME$, TIMER, TO, TROFF, TRON

USING, USR

VAL, VARPTR, VARPTR$, VIEW

WAIT, WEND, WHILE, WIDTH, WINDOW, WRITE, WRITE#

XOR

APPENDIX E

SUMMARY OF BASIC FUNCTIONS

The more commonly used Microsoft BASIC functions are as follows.

ABS

returns the absolute value of its argument:

PRINT ABS (−2.34)
 2.34

ASC

returns the ASCII code for the first character in its argument, which must be of string type (see Appendix F for the ASCII codes), e.g.

PRINT ASC("ABCD")
 65

ATN

returns the arctangent (in radians) of its argument.

CDBL

converts its argument to a double precision number.

CHR$

converts an ASCII code to its character equivalent, e.g.

PRINT CHR$(65)
A

CHR$ may be used to produce special effects on the printer or the screen, e.g.

PRINT CHR$(7)

will beep the speaker.

CINT

converts its argument to an integer by rounding, e.g.

PRINT CINT(45.67); CINT(−2.89)
 46 −3

COS

returns the cosine of its argument (assumed to be in radians).

CSNG

converts its argument to a single precision number.

CSRLIN

returns the current vertical position of the cursor (a value in the range 1 to 25), e.g.

```
CLS
PRINT CSRLIN
 3
```

DATE$

returns or sets the current date, e.g.

```
PRINT DATE$
11-02-1984
```

Note that U.S. format is used: mm-dd-yy. In this form, the date may have been set by the system before entering BASIC. In its second form, DATE$ may be used to reset the date, e.g.

```
10 DATE$ = "8/29/82"
20 PRINT DATE$
RUN
08-29-1982
```

The date may also be entered in the form: "mm-dd-yy"

EOF

returns a true value (-1) if an end of file condition occurs on the file represented by its argument, and a false value (0) otherwise, e.g.

```
50  WHILE NOT EOF( 1 )
     .
     .
90  WEND
```

EXP

raises e to the power x where x is the argument.

FIX

truncates its argument to an integer, i.e. chops off the decimal part, e.g.

```
PRINT FIX( 45.67); FIX( −2.89)
 45 −2
```

FRE

returns the number of bytes in memory that are not being used by BASIC. It requires a dummy argument, e.g.

```
NEW
PRINT FRE( 0 )
 61766
```

HEX$

returns a string which is the hexadecimal representation of the decimal argument, e.g

```
PRINT HEX$( 32 )
20
PRINT HEX$( 1023 )
3FF
```

INPUT$

returns a string of n characters read from the keyboard or from a file:

v$ = INPUT$ (n [, filenum])

INPUT$ enables you to read characters from the keyboard that are significant to the BASIC program editor, like a backspace or carriage return.

INSTR

searches for the first occurrence of string y$ in x$ starting from the nth character:

v = INSTR([n,] x$, y$)

For example,

```
10   A$ = "ABCDEB"
20   B$ = "B"
30   PRINT INSTR( A$, B$); INSTR( 4, A$, B$ )
RUN
 2   6
```

INT

returns the largest integer that is less than or equal to its argument, e.g.

```
PRINT INT( 45.67); INT( −2.89 )
 45 −3
```

LEFT$

returns the leftmost n characters of its string argument, e.g.

```
10 A$ = "NAPOLEON"
20 B$ = LEFT$( A$, 3 )
30 PRINT B$
RUN
NAP
```

LEN

returns the number of characters in its string argument, e.g.

```
PRINT LEN( "NAPOLEON" )
 8
```

LOF

returns the number of bytes allocated to the file represented by its argument (length of the file).

LOG

returns the natural logarithm of its argument.

MID$

returns the requested part of a given string, or replaces a portion of one string with another string:

v$ = MID$(x$, n [, m])

or

MID$(v$, n [, m]) = y$

In the first form the function returns a string of m characters from x$ starting with the nth character. If m is omitted all the rightmost characters beginning from the nth are returned. In the second form the characters of v$, beginning with the nth character, are replaced by the first m characters of the string y$. If m is omitted all the characters of y$ are used. E.g.

```
10  A$ = "NAPOLEON BONAPARTE"
20  B$ = MID$( A$, 5, 4 )
30  MID$( A$, 13 ) = "Y"
40  PRINT A$
50  PRINT B$
RUN
NAPOLEON BONYPARTE
LEON
```

OCT$

returns a string representing the octal value of its decimal argument.

POINT

provides information about a point on the screen. In the form

POINT (x, y)

it returns the colour of the point (x; y) on the screen. In the form

POINT n

it returns the x- (n = 0) or y- (n = 1) co-ordinate of the current position.

POS

returns the current horizontal position of the cursor (in the range 1 to 80 if you have an 80 column machine). POS requires a dummy argument, e.g.

```
PRINT POS( 0 )
 1
```

RIGHT$

returns the rightmost n characters of the string x$:

v$ = RIGHT$(x$, n)

For example,

```
10 A$= "NAPOLEON"
20 B$ = RIGHT$( A$, 2 )
30 PRINT B$
RUN
ON
```

RND

returns a random number in the range 0 to 1 exclusive. It may be reseeded in conjucntion with RANDOMIZE and TIMER, e.g the program

```
10   RANDOMIZE TIMER
20   FOR I = 1 TO 10
30      PRINT RND
40   NEXT I
```

will generate a different random sequence whenever it is run. See Chapter Ten for more examples.

SCREEN

returns the ASCII code for the character in the given row and column of the screen. The general form is

a = SCREEN(row, column)

where a is the ASCII code of the character.

SGN

returns the sign of its argument:

v = SGN(x)

where the value 1, 0 or -1 is returned if x is positive, zero, or negative respectively.

SIN

returns the sine of its argument (assumed to be in radians).

SPACE$

returns a string of n spaces, e.g.

```
10   FOR I = 1 TO 5
20      X$ = SPACE$( I )
30      PRINT X$; I
40   NEXT I
```

```
RUN
    1
      2
        3
          4
            5
```

SPC

skips n spaces in a PRINT statement, e.g.

```
PRINT "OVER" SPC( 15 ) "THERE"
OVER                   THERE
```

SQR

returns the square root of its argument.

STR$

returns a string representation of the value of its argument.

STRING$

returns a string of length n whose characters all have ASCII code m or are equal to the first character of x$:

v$ = STRING$(n, m)

or

v$ = STRING$(n, x$)

An example of the first form is:

```
10   X$ = STRING$( 10, 45 )
20   PRINT X$
RUN
----------
```

An example of the second form is:

```
10   X$ = "NAPOLEON"
20   Y$ = STRING$( 5, X$ )
30   PRINT Y$
RUN
NNNNN
```

TAB

tabulates to column n, where n is its argument, i.e. the next item to be printed begins in column n.

TAN

returns the tangent of its argument (assumed to be in radians).

TIME$

returns or sets the current time. In its first form

v$ = TIME$

the current time is returned as an 8 character string of the form "hh:mm:ss". In its second form

TIME$ = x$

the current time is reset according to the value of x$, which must of the form "hh:mm:ss".

TIMER

returns a single precision number representing the number of seconds elapsed since midnight.

VAL

returns the numerical value of its string argument, e.g.

```
10   D$ = "1984"
20   PREV = VAL( D$ ) – 1
30   PRINT PREV
RUN
 1983
```

VAL strips blanks, tabs and line feeds from the argument string before determining the result. Trailing characters which are not numeric are ignored, e.g.

```
PRINT VAL( " 3 CONIFER WAY" )
 3
```

If the first characters of the argument are not numeric, VAL returns the value zero.

APPENDIX F

ASCII CHARACTER CODES

ASCII codes, which define the ASCII lexical collating sequence, use seven bits per character, so there are 128 possible codes, from 0 to 127. Codes 0 to 31 and code 127 are for special non-printing "control" characters. Codes 32 to 126 are for characters that can be printed, and are as follows:

32	(blank)	64	@	96	`
33	!	65	A	97	a
34	"	66	B	98	b
35	#	67	C	99	c
36	$	68	D	100	d
37	%	69	E	101	e
38	&	70	F	102	f
39	'	71	G	103	g
40	(	72	H	104	h
41	)	73	I	105	i
42	*	74	J	106	j
43	+	75	K	107	k
44	,	76	L	108	l
45	—	77	M	109	m
46	.	78	N	110	n
47	/	79	O	111	o
48	0	80	P	112	p
49	1	81	Q	113	q
50	2	82	R	114	r
51	3	83	S	115	s
52	4	84	T	116	t
53	5	85	U	117	u
54	6	86	V	118	v
55	7	87	W	119	w
56	8	88	X	120	x
57	9	89	Y	121	y
58	:	90	Z	122	z
59	;	91	[	123	{
60	<	92	\	124	|
61	=	93	]	125	}
62	>	94	^	126	~
63	?	95	_		

Some of the special control codes are as follows:
 7 beep
 9 tab

10 line feed
11 home
12 form feed
13 carriage return
28 cursor left
27 "escape"
29 cursor right
30 cursor up
31 cursor down

APPENDIX G

USING THE KEYBOARD

Editing a Program

Any line on the screen may be edited as follows.

Move the cursor to the position of the error in the line, using the keys 2, 4, 6 or 8 in the numeric keypad on the right of the keyboard. The keys make the cursor move down, left, right or up respectively. Note that if you keep the key pressed down for more than half a second, the cursor continues to move. This is called "key cycling", and applies to any character key on the keyboard.

If you wish to delete one or more characters in a line, position the cursor under the character to be deleted, and press the **Del** key (bottom right). The offending character(s) will disappear, and the characters to the right will all move one position to the left.

To insert one or more characters in a line, position the cursor under the character in front of which you want to insert, and press the **Ins** key (bottom right). Note that the shape of the cursor changes to indicate that the keyboard is in insert mode. Any characters typed now will be inserted into the line, all characters to the right moving to the right. Insertion continues until any key affecting the cursor is pressed.

N.B. No changes to a line are effective until ® is pressed, i.e. the edited line must be re-entered into the workspace by pressing ®

Special Function Keys

Some keys have special functions, usually when pressed simultaneously with certain other keys, as described below.

Alt/Ctrl/Del

performs a System Reset. This is similar to, but faster than switching the computer off and on again. The **Ctrl** and **Alt** keys must be held down together, after which **Del** should be pressed.

Ctrl/B

prints a message to tell you where the last error occurred.

Ctrl/Break

stops program execution and returns to BASIC command level. It is also used to exit from AUTO (automatic line number generation).

Ctrl/End

erases (on the screen, not from the memory) to the end of the logical line from the current cursor position.

Ctrl/F

moves the cursor to the beginning of the next word to the right.

Ctrl/G

causes the computer to beep.

Ctrl/Home

clears the screen and positions the cursor in the top left corner of the screen.

Ctrl/M

moves the cursor to the first column of the next line.

Ctrl/N

moves the cursor to the bottom left corner of the screen.

Ctrl/NumLock

suspends an operation, like printing, listing, or executing. Press any alphanumeric or cursor control key to continue the operation.

Ctrl/PrtSc

records on the printer any text appearing on the screen. Press **Ctrl/PrtSc** again to cancel this function (i.e. it operates as a "toggle" switch.

Ctrl/T

switches the function key display on/off.

Ctrl/W

deletes from the current cursor position to the beginning of the next word.

Esc

erases the current logical line from the screen (but not from the memory).

Shift/PrtSc

prints the contents of the screen on the printer.

BASIC Keywords

The **Alt** key pressed with certain letter keys enters a BASIC keyword, e.g. if you press **Alt**/A the word AUTO appears on the screen. Some of the keywords are as follows:

Letter	Keyword
A	AUTO
C	COLOR
D	DELETE
E	ELSE
F	FOR
I	INPUT
N	NEXT
O	OPEN
P	PRINT
R	RUN
S	SCREEN
T	THEN
U	USING (i.e. **Alt**/PU gives PRINT USING)
W	WIDTH

APPENDIX H

SOLUTIONS TO SELECTED PROBLEMS

EXERCISE 1

1.1 110 INPUT A, B
     120 SUM = A + B
     130 DIFF = A − B
     140 PROD = A * B
     150 QUOT = A / B
     160
     170 PRINT "THE SUM IS: "; SUM
     180 PRINT "THE DIFFERENCE IS: "; DIFF
     190 PRINT "THE PRODUCT IS: "; PROD
     200 PRINT "THE QUOTIENT IS: "; QUOT
     210 END

EXERCISES 2

2.2 (a) Comma invalid: should be 9.87
    (b) Valid
    (c) Valid
    (d) Invalid: integer may not be less than -32768
    (e) Asterisk invalid: should be 3.57E2
    (f) Valid
    (g) Valid, though plus is unnecessary
    (h) Comma invalid: should be 3.57E-2

2.3 (a) Valid
    (b) Valid
    (c) Invalid: first character must be a letter
    (d) Invalid: quote marks are not allowed
    (e) Valid!
    (f) Invalid: asterisk is not allowed
    (g) Valid
    (h) Invalid: plus is not allowed
    (i) Valid: ! specifies (the default) single precision type
    (j) Invalid: NAME is a reserved word ($ is the type declaration character)
    (k) Invalid: reserved word
    (l) Valid: % is the integer type declaration character

2.4 (a) P + W / U
    (b) P + W / (U + V)
    (c) (P + W / (U + V)) / (P + W / (U − V))
    (d) X * X
    (e) X ^ 2.5
    (f) X ^ 0.5

(g) X ^ (Y + Z)
(h) X ^ Y ^ Z
(i) X ^ (Y ^ Z)
(j) X − X ^ 3 / (3 * 2) + X ^ 5 / (5 * 4 * 3 * 2)
(k) (− B + (B * B − 4 * A * C) ^ 0.5) / (2 * A)

2.5 (a) I = I + 1
(b) I = I ^ 3 + J
(c) IF E > F THEN G = E ELSE G = F
(d) IF D > 0 THEN X = − B
(e) IF I MOD 2 = 0 THEN X = − X
(f) K = I MOD J

2.7 100 REM CONVERSION OF FAHRENHEIT TO CENTIGRADE
    110
    120 INPUT TEMPF
    130 TEMPC = 5 * (TEMPF − 32) / 9
    140 PRINT TEMPC; " DEGREES CENTIGRADE"
    150 END

2.8 100 REM CONVERSION OF CENTIGRADE TO FAHRENHEIT
    110
    120 INPUT TEMPC
    130 TEMPF = 9 * TEMPC / 5 + 32
    140 PRINT TEMPF; " DEGREES FAHRENHEIT"
    150 END

2.10 ...
    100 TEMP = A
    110 A = B
    120 B = TEMP

2.11 ...
    100 A = A − B
    110 B = B + A
    120 A = B − A

2.12 A = 4; X = 1 + 1/2 + 1/3 + 1/4

2.13 100 X = 0
    110 FOR A = 1 TO 4
    120   X = X + 1 / A
    130 NEXT A

2.14 The limit is π.

2.17 100 REM FUTURE VALUE OF ANNUITY
    105
    110 INPUT "D, R (%), N, K"; D, R, N, K
    120 R = R / 100
    130 V = D * ((1 + R / N) ^ (N * K) − 1) / (R / N)
    140 END

EXERCISES 3

3.1 You should get a picture of tangents to a curve.

3.2 (a) 4

(b) 2

(c) The algorithm (attributed to Euclid!) finds the HCF (Highest common factor) of two numbers by using the fact that the HCF divides exactly into the difference between the two numbers, and that if the numbers are equal, the HCF is equal to them.

EXERCISES 4

4.2   1. Input a, b, c, d, e, f
     2. $u = ae - db$
     3. $v = ec - bf$
     4. If $u \neq 0$ then
         4.1. $x = (ec - bf)/u$
         4.2. $y = (af - dc)/u$
         4.3. Print x, y
     5. If $u = 0$ and $v = 0$ then
         5.1. Print "Lines coincide"
     6. If $u = 0$ and $v \neq 0$ then
         6.1. Print "Lines are parallel".

```
100  REM SOLUTION OF SIMULTANEOUS LINEAR EQUATIONS
110
120  INPUT A, B, C, D, E, F
130  U = A * E - D * B
140  V = E * C - B * F
150  IF U <> 0 THEN GOSUB 500
160  IF U = 0 AND V = 0 THEN PRINT "LINES COINCIDE"
170  IF U = 0 AND V <> 0 THEN PRINT "LINES ARE PARALLEL"
180  STOP
190
500  REM COMPUTE X AND Y CO-ORDINATES OF SOLUTION
510  X = (E * C - B * F) / U
520  Y = (A * F - D * C) / U
530  PRINT X, Y
540  RETURN
550
990  END
```

EXERCISES 5

5.1   For a given interest rate, the time to double is always the same, no matter what the initial balance is. This is a general feature of what is called geometric or exponential growth.

5.2
```
100  SUM = 0
110  FOR J = 1 TO 100
120     SUM = SUM + J
130  NEXT J
140  PRINT SUM
```

5.3
```
100  SUM = 0
110  FOR J = 1 TO 100
120     SUM = SUM + 1 / J
```

SOLUTIONS TO SELECTED PROBLEMS

```
       130  NEXT J
       140  PRINT SUM

5.4    100  SUM = 0
       110  I = 0
       120  WHILE SUM < 100
       130    ANS = SUM
       140    INTS = I
       150    I = I + 1
       160    SUM = SUM + I
       170  WEND
       180  PRINT "SUM:       "; ANS
       190  PRINT "INTEGERS: "; INTS
       200  END

5.5a   100  REM EASY AS PI!
       110
       120  PI = 1
       130  INPUT N
       140  FOR K = 1 TO N
       150    PI = PI + ( -1 ) ^ K / (2 * K + 1)
       160  NEXT K
       170  PI = 4 * PI
       180  PRINT "PI ="; PI; " AFTER"; N; " TERMS"
       190  END

5.5b   100  REM PI AGAIN
       110
       120  PI = 0
       130  INPUT N
       140  FOR K = 1 TO N
       150    PI = PI + 1 / (4 * K - 3) / (4 * K - 1)
       160  NEXT K
       170  PI = 8 * PI
       180  PRINT "PI ="; PI; " AFTER"; N; " TERMS"
       190  END

5.6    10   REM THE LIMIT e
       20
       30   X = 0.1
       40   FOR I = 1 TO 5
       50     E = 1 / ( (1 - X) ^ (1 / X) )
       60     PRINT X; E
       70     X = X / 10
       80   NEXT I
       90   END

5.8    100  REM SUMS THE TAYLOR WAY
       110
       120  INPUT X              '( X = 1 MAKES IT SUM TO e!)
       130  EX = 1
       140  ER = 1E-6
       150  K = 1
       160  TERM = 1
       170
       180  WHILE ABS(TERM) >= ER
       190    TERM = TERM * X / K
       200    EX = EX + TERM
```

```
210     K + K + 1
220 WEND
230
240 PRINT X; EX; EXP( X )
250 END
```

5.9
```
100 REM COMPOUND INTEREST IN THE LIMIT
105
110 INPUT "A, R (%), K: ", A, R, K
120 N = 1
130 R = R / 100
140 FOR I = 1 TO 25
150    V = A * (1 + R / N) ^ (N * K)
160    PRINT N; V
170    N = 2 * N
180 NEXT I
```

Note that the output moves away from the limit for N greater than about 250, because rounding error (see Chapter Seven) takes over.

EXERCISES 6

6.1 (a) C = SQR(A * A + B * B)
     (b) THETA = THETA * 3.141593 / 180
         C = SQR(A * A + B * B − 2 * A * B * COS(THETA))

6.2
```
100 REM APPROXIMATELY NORMAL?
110
120 A = 0.4361836
130 B = − 0.1201676
140 C = 0.937298
150 PI = 3.141593
160
170 FOR X = 0 TO 4 STEP 0.1
180    R = EXP( − X * X / 2 ) / SQR( 2 * PI )
190    T = 1 / (1 + 0.3326 * X)
200    PHI = 0.5 − R * (A * T + B * T ^ 2 + C * T ^ 3)
210    PRINT X TAB( 15 ) PHI
220 NEXT X
230
240 END
```

6.3
```
100 REM EXPONENTIAL GROWTH
105
110 INPUT "A, R, K"; A, R, K
120 V = A * EXP( R * K )
130 PRINT V
```

6.4
```
100 REM PERIOD OF LOAN REDEMPTION
110
120 INPUT "A, P, N, R (%)"; A, P, N, R
130 R = R / 100
140 K = LOG( P / (P − R * A / N) ) / LOG( 1 + R / N ) / N
```

EXERCISE 8

8.1 Amend lines 190 and 220, and insert line 195, as follows:

```
190   PRINT USING "###%"; 100 * R;
195   PRINT TAB( 15 )
220      PRINT USING "###.##          "; P;
```

EXERCISES 9

9.1a ...
```
100   FOR I = 0 TO 99
110      NUM( I ) = I
120   NEXT I
```

9.1b ...
```
100   FOR I = 1 TO 50
110      NUM( I ) = 2 * I
120   NEXT I
```

9.2
```
100   REM DECIMAL TO BINARY CONVERSION
110
120   DIM BIN(5)                               'THE BINARY DIGITS
130   INPUT NUM
140   DEC = NUM
150
160   FOR I = 5 TO 1 STEP −1
170      BIN( I ) = NUM MOD 2
180      NUM = NUM \ 2
190   NEXT I
200
210   PRINT USING "DECIMAL:  ####      BINARY: "; DEC;
220   FOR I = 1 TO 5
230      PRINT USING "#"; BIN( I );
240   NEXT I
250   PRINT
260   END
```

9.3 ...
```
100   F(1) = 1
110   F(2) = 1
120   FOR K = 3 TO 100
130      F( K ) = F( K−1 ) + F( K−2 )
140   NEXT K
```

9.4 1. Initialize: $n = 3$; $p(1) = 2$; $j = 1$ (counts the primes)
    2. While $n < 1000$ repeat
       2.1. $i = 1$
       2.2. rem = $mod(n, p(i))$
       2.3. While rem $\neq 0$ and $p(i) < \sqrt{n}$ repeat
          2.3.1. $i = i + 1$
          2.3.2. rem = $mod(n, p(i))$
       2.4. If rem $\neq 0$ then
          2.4.1. $j = j + 1$ (another prime has been found!)
          2.4.2. $p(j) = n$
       2.5. $n = n + 2$ (only test odd numbers for primality)
    3. Print all the $p(j)$s.

9.6
```
100   REM ZELLER'S CONGRUENCE
110
120   DIM DAY$(6)                                  'DAYS OF THE WEEK
130
140   FOR I = 0 TO 6
150      READ DAY$(I)
160   NEXT I
170
180   INPUT DAY, MONTH, YEAR
190   YR = YEAR
200   MON = MONTH − 2
210   IF MON <= 0 THEN MON = MON + 12
220   IF MON >= 11 THEN YR = YR − 1
230   CENT = YR \ 100
240   YR = YR MOD 100
250   F = INT( 2.6 * MON − 0.2) + DAY + YR + INT( YR / 4 )
260   F = F + INT( CENT / 4 ) − 2 * CENT
270   F = F MOD 7
280
290   PRINT USING "##−"; DAY; MONTH;
300   PRINT USING "####: "; YEAR;
310   PRINT DAY$(F)
320
330   DATA SUNDAY,MONDAY,TUESDAY,WEDNESDAY,THURSDAY,FRIDAY
340   DATA SATURDAY
350   END
```

EXERCISES 10

10.2
```
100   REM BINGO!
110
120   DIM BING(99)
130   RANDOMIZE TIMER
140
150   REM PUT THE NUMBERS IN THE BAG
160   FOR I = 1 TO 99
170      BING(I) = I
180   NEXT I
190
200   REM TAKE THEM OUT AGAIN BY 2ND METHOD OF §10.6
210   FOR I = 1 TO 99
220      R = INT( 99 * RND ) + 1
230      SWAP BING(R), BING(I)
240   NEXT I
250
260   REM PRINT THEM NEATLY (10 PER LINE)
270   FOR I = 1 TO 99
280      PRINT USING "###"; BING(I);
290      IF I MOD 10 = 0 THEN PRINT
300   NEXT I
310   END
```

10.3
```
100   REM ESTIMATING PI
110   REM THIS IS A RATHER INEFFICIENT METHOD!
120
130   RANDOMIZE TIMER
140   PI = 0
```

```
150  INPUT NUM                              'NUMBER OF POINTS GENERATED
160
170  FOR I = 1 TO NUM
180     X = RND
190     Y = RND
200     IF X * X + Y * Y < 1 THEN PI = PI + 1
210  NEXT I
220
230  PI = 4 * PI / NUM
240  PRINT USING "PI IS VERY ROUGHLY ##.###"; PI
250  END
```

EXERCISE 11

11.1
```
100  REM DERIVATIVES THE NEWTON WAY
110
120  DEF FNF( X ) = X ^ 3
130  X = 1
140  H = 1
150  FOR I = 1 TO 30
160     DF = (FNF( X+H ) – FNF( X )) / H
170     PRINT H; DF
180     H = H / 2
190  NEXT I
200  END
```

EXERCISES 14

14.1 $x_0 = 1$; $x_1 = 1.333$; $x_2 = 1.2639$; $x_3 = 1.2599$; $x_4 = 1.2599...$

14.2 (a) The real roots are 1.856 and -1.697.
(b) 0.589, 3.096, 6.285 ... (roots get closer to multiples of π)
(c) 1; 2; 5
(d) 1.303
(e) The real roots are 1.768 and 2.241. I couldn't find any more. Can you?

14.3 Successive bisections are: 1.5, 1.25, 1.375, 1.4375 and 1.40625. The exact answer is 1.414214, so the last bisection is within the required error.

14.4 22 (the exact answer is 21.3333)

14.5 $x(1) =$ (a) 0.75, (b) 0.6836 (0.6321 exactly).

14.6 i.e. solve $dy/dx = x^2$ numerically. Answer is 14. (This is effectively the rectangular rule for integration.)

INDEX

! formatting character -56
! type declaration character -11
# formatting character -54
# type declaration character -52
$ type declaration character -21
$$ formatting characters -55
% type declaration character -11
\+ formatting character -55
\\ formatting characters -56
^ formatting character -55
_formatting character -56

Adjacency matrix -106
Algorithm -26
Alphabetical sort -66
AND -20
Animation -95
Area of a polygon -110
Arithmetic memory -4
Arithmetic operator -13
Arithmetic operator: precedence -13
Array -62
Array: element of -62
ASCII -66
Assignment statement -12
AUTO command -9
AUTO command: how to exit -9

Background colour -92
Bacteria division -78, 89
Bacteria growth -129
Bar chart -63
Binomial coefficient -41
Bisection method -119
Bit -11
Blinking text -92
Border colour -92
Bubble sort -64
Budget program -72
Bug -50
Byte -11

CASE structure -35
CIRCLE statement -93
CLOSE statement -57
CLS command -9
Co-ordinate transformation -104

Collating sequence -66
COLOR statement -92
Colour text -92
Concatenation -22
Constant -10

DATA statement -20
Dealing a hand of cards -83
Debugging -50
Decile -63
DEF FN statement -90
DEFDBL statement -52
DEFINT statement -11
DEFSTR statement -21
DELETE command -9
Determinant of a matrix -110
DIM statement -62
Direct mode -50
Diskette file -7
Double precision -52
DRAW statement -94

Editing a program -163
EOF function -58
EQV -20
Euler's method -125
Execution error -51
Exponent -10

Factorial -40
False -20
FIFO queue -85
File: data -56
File: program -7
File: random access -75
File: sequential -75
Filename -8
FILES command -8
Fixed point constant -10
Floating point constant -10
Flowchart -26
FOR-NEXT statement -15
FOR-NEXT statement: full definition -41
Formatting character -54
Free fall against air resistance -125
Frequency distribution -63
Function: user defined -90

GET statement -95
Global variable -34
GOSUB statement -33
GOTO statement -40
Graph: on line printer -97
Graphics: high resolution -96
Graphics: interactive -96
Graphics: medium resolution -93

IF-THEN-ELSE statement -18
IMP -20
Inline comment -6
INPUT # statement -59
INPUT statement -14
Integer constant -10
Interactive graphics -96
Interpreter -50

KEY statement -95
KILL command -8

Largest Number in a List -35
LEFT$ function -75
Lexical collating sequence -66
LINE INPUT # statement -58
LINE statement -95
List -62
LIST command -9
LLIST command -9
LOAD command -7
LOCATE statement -98
Logarithmic spiral -99
Logical expression -20
Logical operator -20
LPRINT statement -7
LPRINT USING statement -56

Machine code -50
Mantissa -10
MAT statements -112
Matrix -100
Matrix multiplication -102
Mean of a set of numbers -61
MERGE command -104
MOD operator -13

NAME command -59

Network -105
NEW command -9
Newton quotient -124
Newton's method -115
Newton's method: solving an equation -91
Non-executable statement -11
NOT -20
Numerical differentiation -124
Numerical evaluation of integrals -122
Numerical method -115
Numerical solution of differential equations -125
Numerical solution of equations -115

OPEN FOR APPEND -72
OPEN FOR INPUT -58
OPEN FOR OUTPUT -57
OPEN statement -57
OPTION BASE statement -62
OR -20
Order of merit list -67
Overlay -137

PAINT statement -93
Precedence of operators -13
Predator prey model -132
PRINT # statement -59
PRINT statement -6
PRINT USING statement -54
PRINT USING: strings -56
Print zone -7
Printing a program -9
Printing output of a program -6
Program memory -4
Programming style -7
Projectile motion -48
Protected program -152
PSET statement -94
PUT statement -96

Queue simulation -85

Radian measure -47
Random access file -75
Random number generator -77
Random walk -79
RANDOMIZE statement -77

INDEX

Reachability matrix -105
READ statement -20
READ-AHEAD structure -39
Recursion -90
Relational operator -19
REM statement -5
RENUM command -9
Reserved word -11
RETURN statement -33
RND function -77
Rolling a die -77
Rounding error -52
RUN command -9
Runge-Kutta method -132

SAVE command -7
SCREEN statement -92
Seeding the random number generator -77
Sequential file -75
Simulation -77
Simulation: a random walk -79
Simulation: bacteria division -78
Simulation: dealing a hand of cards -83
Simulation: queues -85
Simulation: rolling a die -77
Simulation: spinning a coin -79
Simulation: traffic flow -80
Single precision -11
Sorting numbers -64
Sorting words -66
SPACE$ function -60
Spinning a coin -79
Standard deviation of a set of numbers -61
String concatenation -22
String variable -21

Structure plan -3
Subroutine -33
Subscript -62
Subscripted variable -62
Sunflower seeds -95
SWAP statement -66
Syntax error -50
SYSTEM command -9

TAB function -7
Text mode -92
TIMER function -77
Trace debugging facility -51
Traffic flow simulation -80
Transformation of co-ordinates -104
Trapezoidal rule -122
TROFF command -51
TRON command -51
True -20
Type declaration character -11

User defined function -90

Variable -4
Variable name -11
Variable: string -21
Vertical motion under gravity -12
Volume of excavation -108

WHILE-WEND statements -39
WIDTH statement -92
Workspace -4
WRITE # statement -57
WRITE statement -59

XOR -20

NOTES

NOTES

NOTES

NOTES